A BREACH OF IMPUNITY

T0339103

American Association
for the INTERNATIONAL COMMISSION OF JURISTS, Inc.
777 United Nations Plaza, New York, New York 10017

ELI WHITNEY DEBEVOISE
(1899–1990)
Chairman Emeritus

Directors:

DONALD T. FOX
Chairman of the Board

WILLIAM J. BUTLER
President

HARVEY J. GOLDSCHMID
Secretary

P. NICHOLAS KOURIDES
Treasurer

ROBERT P. BASS, JR.	RICHARD H. MOORE
ANDREA BONIME-BLANC	ANDRE W. G. NEWBURG
CONRAD K. HARPER	STEPHEN A. OXMAN
PETER S. HELLER	JEROME J. SHESTACK
GEORGE N. LINDSAY	PETER O. A. SOLBERT
SHEILA AVRIN MCLEAN	EDWARD HALLAM TUCK

Directors Emeriti:

DUDLEY B. BONSAL

WHITNEY NORTH SEYMOUR
(1901–1983)

BENJAMIN R. SHUTE
(1911–1986)

BETHUEL M. WEBSTER
(1900–1989)

A BREACH OF IMPUNITY

*The Trial for the Murder
of Jesuits in El Salvador*

REPORT OF THE TRIAL OBSERVER OF THE

INTERNATIONAL COMMISSION
OF JURISTS

FORDHAM UNIVERSITY PRESS
New York
1992

Copyright © 1992 by Fordham University
All rights reserved
ISBN 0-8232-1443-5
LC 92-26144

Originally published in Spanish (*El Salvador: Una Brecha a la Impunidad*) in 1991 by the
International Commission of Jurists

Library of Congress Cataloging-in-Publication Data

Artucio, Alejandro.
[El Salvador, English]
A breach of impunity : the trial for the murder of Jesuits in El Salvador : report of the
observer of the International Commission of Jurists.
p. cm.
Translation of: El Salvador.
ISBN 0-8232-1443-5
1. Benavides Moreno, Guillermo Alfredo—Trials, litigation, etc.
2. Trials (Murder)—El Salvador. 3. Trials (Terrorism)—El
Salvador. 4. Jesuits—El Salvador. I. International Commission of
Jurists (1952–) II. Title.
KGC135.J47A77 1992
345.7284'02523—dc20
[347.284052523] 92-26144
CIP

Printed in the United States of America

CONTENTS

FOREWORD

The 1989 murder of six Jesuit priests and two of their household family at the Central American University (UCA) in San Salvador stunned even those who were familiar with the brutal violence of the Salvadoran Civil War. The eight, murdered in the early morning of November 16, joined the litany of 70,000 other men, women, and children who had been killed in a war of attrition that has spanned a dozen years.

The Jesuits of the UCA were not the first religious figures to be victims of the conflict. In 1977, their friend and brother Jesuit, Father Rutilio Grande, s.j., was ambushed on his way to his Sunday pastoral duties. In March of 1980, the heroic Archbishop of San Salvador, Oscar Romero, was slain by an assassin's bullet while celebrating Mass. In December of that year, four U.S. churchwomen were kidnapped, assaulted, and murdered as they returned from the San Salvador airport.

But unlike many previous killings the murders on the UCA campus set off a storm of outrage that could not be silenced by the routine evasions of government officials. Spokesmen in Washington, as well as in San Salvador, first suggested that the murders were probably the work of FMLN guerrillas, but international pressure finally led to an admission by President Cristiani on January 8, 1990, that "some elements of the Armed Forces" had been involved in the killings. Eight members of the Salvadoran military were then charged with the crimes, including a colonel, the highest-ranking officer ever to be so accused.

When I visited San Salvador in February 1990, along with several other U.S. Jesuit university presidents, we were told by both U.S. and Salvadoran authorities that the murders had been an aberrant violation of the standards of the Salvadoran military. For this reason there was little official interest, it appeared, in determining who were the "intellectual authors of the crime," as the Salvadoran Jesuits kept asking.

The course of the investigation that followed, chronicled in the report of the Moakley Congressional Task Force, made it clear that the executions of November 16 were not isolated acts of eight renegade soldiers. Carried out in darkness on the campus of a Catholic university within hailing distance of the Salvadoran command headquarters, the November UCA massacre was the work of a military establishment that believed it could operate with reckless impunity in a society where a flawed system of justice made a mockery of human rights.

The present volume represents a study by the International Commission of Jurists of the trial, eventually held in San Salvador in September 1991, of the eight men accused of the UCA killings. It is aptly titled *A Breach of Impunity*. The study concludes that justice was not achieved in this trial; indeed, justice probably could not have been achieved. But the wall that has insulated the Salvadoran military from the claims of justice has been broken.

This is the story of a flawed system of justice, but it is also the story of valiant individuals—prosecutors and jurists—who sought to serve the cause of justice, despite the crippling system in which they worked and the ominous dangers with which they had to live.

I am pleased that the Fordham University Press has been able to publish this sobering story, and I congratulate the International Commission of Jurists for the dedication to justice and human rights reflected in this document. Through the publication of this book the Jesuits and our colleagues at Fordham University express again our admiration for and solidarity with our Jesuit brothers and their colleagues at the Central American University in San Salvador.

New York, October 1992   JOSEPH A. O'HARE, S.J.
                                                          President
                                                  Fordham University

PREFACE

The International Commission of Jurists sent its Legal Officer for Latin America, Dr. Alejandro Artucio, as an observer to the trial held in San Salvador concerning the assassination of six Jesuit priests, the cook at their residence, and her daughter. The savage murders had occurred November 16, 1989 in the residence of the Jesuits, located on the campus of the Central American University "José Simeón Cañas," and was accompanied by serious damages to the premises, highly destructive weapons have been used in the attack. Two years later, in September 1991, the public phase of the trial was conducted, which our observer attended.

The report which we are now publishing goes beyond an analysis of the trial. It provides an overview of the country and describes the political and social context in which the assassinations occurred and in which the trial was held.

Important changes are occurring in El Salvador as a result of peace negotiations undertaken under the sponsorship of the United Nations Secretary General between the Government of the Republic and the Farabundo Martí Front for National Liberation (Frente Farabundo Martí para la Liberación Nacional–FMLN). These negotiations have reached an advanced stage; one result has been an accord permitting the presence, in El Salvador, of ONUSAL, a United Nations mission charged with verifying respect for human rights and fundamental liberties. According to our observer, the peace negotiations, even if they have not yet succeeded in bringing a halt to the fighting, have created enormous hope in the population, weary of eleven years of civil war and its attendant suffering.

The victims of the assassinations of November 1989 were, in their majority, distinguished personalities, recognized not only in El Salvador but in other countries as well. They were teachers at the Central American University, and they were Jesuit priests.

Their deaths caused considerable impact around the world and focused close attention on El Salvador. Divers bodies, including the UN Commission on Human Rights and its Subcommission, various national parliaments, numerous nongovernmental organizations, and political and religious personalities throughout the world spoke up to demand that justice be done.

The report describes in minute detail the military precision with which these crimes were prepared and executed. The way in which they were carried out demonstrates the extreme dangerousness of the perpetrators and the contempt for legality on the part of a group of military personnel who, following the crime, did everything possible to place the blame for it on elements of the FMLN. For reasons cited in this report, the deed could only have been carried out if its participants were convinced of being able to act with total impunity.

Personal details are provided concerning the authors of the crime—a group of commandos from the Atlacatl Rapid Reaction Battalion, an elite unit trained and tested in counterinsurgency warfare. The report also describes the different stages of the criminal proceedings, the obstacles encountered, and the conduct of the police bodies charged with the investigation, as well as that of the Armed Forces, the judge, the office of the General Prosecutor, the defense attorneys, and the attorneys for the victims' families.

The report analyzes one by one the criminal charges formulated against the nine military personnel implicated in the crime, in the light both of Salvadoran law and of international law applicable in El Salvador. In addition, the report analyzes the constitutional norms and closely examines the Criminal Code (CP) and the Code of Criminal Procedure (CPP).

The report describes the manner in which the public trial, attended in full by the ICJ observer, was conducted. It presents the extensive discussions and arguments of the various parties, pointing up the marked aggressiveness of the defense counsels against individual persons, institutions, foreign governments, and international observers present at the trial. It also reports and comments on the verdict issued by a jury of the people, with which the trial concluded. The jury found only two defendants guilty of murder and acquitted the other seven. It also acquitted all nine of the defendants on the charges of the crime of terrorism.

In the opinion of the observer, the verdict ignored the system incorporated in the Criminal Code and the Code of Criminal Procedure with regard to the norms governing criminal responsibility, the circumstances modifying such responsibility, and the validity of documentary evidence. The observer does not hesitate to qualify the verdict as "arbitrary" and "surprising," since during the investigative phase the accused had confessed extensively, in specific detail, and in concordance with one another about their respective roles in the action. In their confessions they admitted clearly their responsibility in what the judge appropriately called crimes of murder and terrorism. And these confessions were not validly discredited during the trial.

The observer devotes the last chapter of the report to his conclusions and final appraisal. He points to the facts which, in his opinion, were fully proved and which would have justified the condemnation of all of the accused before any tribunal of law. He summarizes the performance of the various parties and of the jury during the public trial. In providing a global assessment of the trial, the observer concludes that the trial itself was not just, because its outcome was not just; and that the investigation had been limited from the very beginning, which necessarily would condition the manner in which the truth was sought.

Despite these criticisms, the observer considers the fact that such a trial was held at all to contain a number of positive aspects which, it is to be hoped, will contribute to a greater respect for human rights in the future. The trial constituted a breach in "the massive wall of impunity" which had been permitting violations of human rights in El Salvador. It was the first time in the recent history of the country that officers of the Salvadoran army had been tried and convicted for having violated human rights. The trial likewise contained an element of "high educational value" for the population, as it was given unusually extensive coverage by the national television, radio, and press. But the final result clearly "was not a triumph of justice."

Finally, the observer recommends modifications to judicial

procedure and particularly to the norms governing the functioning of the jury, and to forensic practices. It is hoped that such modifications could achieve a more adequate working of the administration of justice.

The ICJ observer acknowledges the invaluable cooperation rendered to him by the Lawyers Commitee for Human Rights in New York and the Institute for Human Rights of the Central American University (IDHUCA), facilitating his documentation of the trial and providing him with the necessary logistical support in San Salvador to thoroughly explore the background details of the case, although he maintained his independence of judgment at all times.

I wish to emphasize finally the gratitude of the International Commission of Jurists to the Salvadoran authorities for having granted our observer all of the facilities that made his delicate mission possible.

Geneva, November 1991   ADAMA DIENG
                                                        Secretary General

Chapter 1
THE BACKGROUND

The Country

Smallest country in the region, with some 22,000 km² and a population of approximately 6 million inhabitants, El Salvador is the most densely populated country on the continent.

The subsoil is of volcanic origin and there are various active volcanos. The geography is shaped by a succession of wooded highlands, which in some parts reach altitudes of more than 3,000 meters. Various large rivers cut across valleys lying between mountains. The climate is tropical, with the dry season clearly distinguished from the rainy one; very hot temperatures prevail in the low-lying zones, varying between 22 and 32 degrees centigrade throughout the year; somewhat lower temperatures exist at higher elevations.

Tropical forests abound, with lush vegetation, covering large stretches and containing good timber and an abundance of fruits. The most important crops are coffee, corn, cotton, and fruits. Cattle raising occupies a relatively important place. El Salvador possesses a long coast along the Pacific Ocean, offering good fishing possibilities, though for the moment this resource is little exploited.

El Salvador borders Guatemala, Honduras, Nicaragua, and the Pacific Ocean.

El Salvador has the highest percentage of infant mortality in Central America. Although official statistics are unavailable, various studies put the rates of illiteracy at 17% in the urban sector and 38% in the countryside. Living conditions are difficult for a majority of the population, with a high percentage living below acceptable levels and even in extreme poverty.

The Republic of El Salvador became an independent state in 1841; previously it had formed part of the Central American Federation, which had achieved independence from Spain. The prevailing political Constitution was adopted in 1983 and establishes a system of republican, democratic, and representative government, with three basic organs: the Legislative, the Executive, and the Judicial (Arts. 85 and 86). Currently several modifications to this text are being undertaken, decided in the framework of the peace negotiations being pursued between the Government and the FMLN.

The Constitution accords considerable importance to civil, political, economic, social, and cultural rights. By Art. 144 it establishes that "International treaties concluded by El Salvador with other states or with international organizations constitute laws of the Republic. . . . The law cannot modify or abolish that which has been agreed upon in a treaty currently valid for El Salvador. In the case of conflict between the treaty and a law, the treaty prevails." What the treaty cannot do is to contradict the Constitution; in such a case the said dispositions would be declared inapplicable.

The official language is Spanish (Art. 62).

The Political and Social Context in Which the Assassination of the Jesuits Occurred

Civil War developed at the beginning of the 1980s and has caused some 75,000 victims. The current government was elected at the beginning of 1989, in elections marked by a high rate of abstention (62%). The winner, Alfredo Cristiani, candidate of the ARENA party, took office as President on June 1, 1989. In the preceding years, prior to the presidency of the Christian Democrat José Napoleón Duarte, the country had suffered a succession of governments imposed by force and led by military officers.

The situation of human rights and their systematic violation in El Salvador have preoccupied the international community since the beginning of the 1980s. The Inter-American Commission of Human Rights (ICHR-OAS) has published various reports indicating its concern regarding El Salvador. The United Nations Commission on Human Rights has maintained a watchful eye on the situation since 1980 through the annual reports submitted to it by its Special Representative designated for this purpose, Professor José Antonio Pastor Ridruejo. In view of the gravity of the situation, the mandate of the Special Representative has been reconfirmed year after year by the Commission on Human Rights, with specific approval from the General Assembly. Both the ICHR and the Special Representative have pointed to numerous summary or arbitrary executions, assassinations (including that of Msgr. Oscar Arnulfo Romero, Archbishop of San Salvador), forced disappearances, and cases of torture, committed both by the security forces of the state as well as by "death squads" organized by the extreme right with the participation of military personnel. For its part, the FMLN has been accused of committing kidnappings to obtain money and of destroying components of the economic infrastructure such as electrical power pylons, bridges, etc. Both sides have been charged with violations of humanitarian law, particularly Protocol II, of 1977, supplementary to the Geneva Convention of 1949, and Art. 3 of this Convention.

The combatants in the civil war are, on the one side, the Government, very influenced by the Armed Forces, who continue to wield a considerable share of power, and on the other side the Farabundo Martí Front for National Liberation (FMLN), created in October 1980 on the basis of a union of five guerrilla organizations. The FMLN maintains a military presence and controls, more or less permanently, various areas of the country, particularly in the north and the east; it also carries out incursions into other zones from which it later retreats under pressure from the Armed Forces.

In order to adequately appreciate the political context in which the events occurred, it is very important to remember the military offensive launched by the FMLN at that time. On October 31, 1989, a never-identified group of right-wing extremists detonated a bomb at the headquarters of the National Trade Union Federation of Salvadoran Workers (Federación Nacional Sindical de Trabajadores Salvadoreños—FENASTRAS), killing ten trade union leaders who were having lunch there and wounding 30 persons. Following this attack, the FMLN withdrew from the ongoing peace negotiations with the Government (see below) and launched the largest military offensive of the eleven-year-old civil war.

At 8:00 P.M. on November 11, 1989 the FMLN simultaneously attacked the capital, San Salvador, and the cities of Santa Ana, San Miguel, Zacatecoluca, and Usulután, as well as various army positions in rural areas. Several thousand guerrilla troops entered San Salvador (a city of some 2 million inhabitants), launching simultaneous attacks against a series of military objectives, such as army barracks, the headquarters of the military General Staff, etc.

During the early hours of November 12th, the Government declared a state of siege, including a curfew from 6:00 P.M. to 6:00 A.M. The television, radio, and press, who had been reporting widely on the fighting, were forced to submit to the direction of the Armed Forces television and radio channel Cuscatlán.

There followed intense urban combat, and by the night of November 15th the course of the war had reached a possible turning point, as the Armed Forces found themselves on the verge of being overrun and incapable of dislodging the guerrilla fighters from the working-class districts of the capital in which they had entrenched themselves and where they enjoyed the sympathy of the population, who provided them with food and clothing. That night a meeting was held, involving the participation of the 30 highest military officers in the country, in which it was decided "to raise the level of the war." From this moment on, the machine-gunning of the working-class neighborhoods by the air force intensified, as did the bombing of cities such as San Miguel, causing thousands of deaths among the noncombatant civilian population and the damage or destruction of some 20,000 dwellings.

It was subsequently alleged during the trial, among the specific accusations, that in this high-level meeting it was also decided that certain "ideologues" and "intellectual ringleaders" of the subversion would be eliminated. This included, it was said, the six Jesuit priests who were assassinated the next morning. Nevertheless the lawyers did not provide any proof for their affirmations.

The importance of the offensive can be seen—and this also

explains the climate reigning at that moment—in the fact that the troops of the FMLN only withdrew from the capital after 14 days, and maintained additional sporadic attacks for some days following. These new movements included shifting their positions from the working-class quarters of the city to upper-class neighborhoods where the army would not attack, and from there occupying the Hotel Sheraton, where the visiting Secretary General of the Organization of American States, João Baena Soares, and a group of American military advisors were staying.

The Political Context in Which the Trial Was Held

The war continues, and each day produces new victims. Nevertheless, important progress toward peace has been made on the basis of negotiations which are now taking place as the result of agreements—known as Esquipulas II—reached by the five Central American presidents in 1987 and aimed at achieving peace in the region.

As noted above, peace discussions initiated in San José, Costa Rica, and later continued in Quito, Ecuador, were interrupted in 1989 as a result of the deadly bomb attack perpetrated against the headquarters of FENASTRAS in San Salvador. The major offensive by the FMLN in November 1989 demonstrated that a military solution to the war would be very difficult to achieve, and that the fighting would continue to cause incalculable damage to the population, resulting in further murder and intolerance as well as destruction of the infrastructure and the economy in a country already impoverished.

The peace negotiations between the Government and the FMLN were resumed in 1990, leading to the Geneva Accords on April 4th, those of Caracas on May 21st, and the signing of the Accord on Human Rights, July 26, 1990 in San José, Costa Rica. There followed the Mexico City Accords on April 27, 1991, in which a series of constitutional reforms were accepted, the New York Accord on September 25, 1991, and the cease-fire negotiations, which are set to begin as this report is being written.

The San José Accord on Human Rights led to the setting up in El Salvador on July 26, 1991, of ONUSAL, a one-year "verification" mission by the United Nations charged with monitoring respect for and observance of human rights and fundamental liberties. ONUSAL has now produced its first report for the UN Secretary General (Doc. A/45/1055, S/23037, 16/Set/91). We should mention in passing that the peace negotiations and the presence of the United Nations in the country to monitor respect for rights and liberties has created a sense of enormous hope and expectation among the Salvadoran population that peace may finally be achieved—a climate of hope that the ICJ observer himself witnessed in El Salvador.

Despite the important advances registered in the search for a "definitive and lasting peace," the armed confrontation continued at the time of the trial, with all its consequent tension, agitation, and intolerance. In this connection it is fitting to emphasize that the assassination operation was conducted by the Atlacatl Rapid Reaction Battalion, an elite unit of the Salvadoran army which has benefited from preferential treatment in regard to arms, instruction, and training in military schools in the United States. Atlacatl contains the army's most effective commando units trained in counterinsurgency fighting. Although the indictment itself was very positive, considering that this battalion had participated on numerous occasions in the massacre of peasants in rural areas, for many observers the very fact that the indicted officers belonged to the Atlacatl Battalion would make it difficult for justice to be reached in this case. According to this point of view, the Armed Forces would not tolerate that "its fighting morale be affected" by the sanctioning of soldiers and officers tested in the war. As we will see later, these predictions proved to be not far from the truth. Finally, the context of the war determined from the outset the manner in which the investigation was conducted and later also the result of the trial.

THE VICTIMS[1]

Ignacio Ellacuría Beascoechea, s.j. A world-renowned philosopher and theologian, Father Ellacuría was born in 1930 in

---

[1] The biographical data concerning the victims, the resumé of the actions leading up to and shaping the assassinations, and the description of the accused have been drawn

the Basque country and entered the Society of Jesus in 1947. In 1948 he was sent to El Salvador to continue his novitiate. After taking his first vows, Father Ellacuría studied classical languages, the humanities, and philosophy in Quito, Ecuador (1949–1955). Subsequently he taught philosophy for three years at the seminary of San José de la Montaña in San Salvador. From 1958 to 1962 he pursued theological studies in Innsbruck, Austria and was ordained as a priest there in 1961. In 1962 he began his doctoral studies in philosophy at the Universidad Complutense in Madrid.

Father Ellacuría returned to El Salvador in 1967 and began to teach at the recently established Central American University (Universidad Centroamericana—UCA), to which he increasingly dedicated his time, labor, and devotion. Today the University is in large part an expression of his vision, as much in the design of its campus as in its lines of research, teaching, and social planning. On the occasion of the tenth anniversary of the UCA he wrote, "In the process of liberation of the peoples of Latin America, the university cannot do everything, but what it has to do is indispensable. And if it fails in this undertaking, then it has failed as a university and has betrayed its historic mission."

At the time of his death, Father Ellacuría was rector of the UCA, a post he assumed in 1979. He was also vice-rector of social planning as well as professor of philosophy and theology, and directed the University's cultural extension review, *Estudios Centroamericanos* (*ECA*).

From the very beginning of the armed conflict in El Salvador, Father Ellacuría appealed insistently for a negotiated solution to the civil war, provoking at some points the anger both of the right and the left. During the course of the 1980s, he became one of the most visionary analysts of the national reality in El Salvador. On various occasions he served as a formal or infor-

---

from publications by the Lawyers Committee for Human Rights (New York) and the Instituto de Derechos Humanos de la Universidad Centroamericana "José Simeón Cañas" (IDHUCA) (San Salvador), to whom the International Commission of Jurists wishes to express its appreciation. The documentation provided by these sources made this report possible. These data were compared by the observer with the documentation from the judicial process itself.

mal mediator between the FMLN and the Government. Thus, in 1985 Father Ellacuría and Archbishop Rivera y Damas obtained the release of the daughter of President Duarte, who had been kidnapped by the FMLN. Perhaps because of his effectiveness, Father Ellacuría was a particular target of the Salvadoran right, which regularly referred to him as "nefarious and satanic." In the middle of 1986, the deputies of ARENA (the party of the current Government) launched a campaign in the legislative assembly to strip him of his Salvadoran citizenship, which he had obtained in 1975.

Ignacio Martín-Baró, s.j.   Father Martín-Baró was born in Valladolid, Spain, in 1942. He entered the Society of Jesus in 1959 and, like Ellacuría, was sent to El Salvador to complete his novitiate. From 1961 to 1966 he studied classical languages, the humanities, and philosophy in Ecuador and Colombia. Father Martín-Baró returned to El Salvador in 1966 and taught for a year in the Jesuit secondary school Externado San José and subsequently at the UCA. During the 1970s he studied theology and psychology in Europe as well as at the UCA. In 1979 he obtained a doctorate in psychology from the University of Chicago.

At the time of his death, "Father Nacho," as he was called, was the vice-rector of academics and of research at the UCA, as well as head of the Department of Psychology and a member of the editorial board of the *Estudios Centroamericanos* and the University's psychology review. He was also a founding director of the IUDOP, the only institute of public opinion in El Salvador, during whose first three years he conducted 25 polls concerning such issues as health, employment, democracy, and the war. Father Martín-Baró was also pastor of Jayaque, a rural parish.

Segundo Montes Mozo, s.j.   Born in Valladolid in 1933, Father Montes was sent to El Salvador in 1951 to complete his novitiate. He studied at the Universities of Madrid, Innsbruck, and Quito, and during his first years as a professor taught physics at the Externado San José. He was the rector of this school from 1973 to 1976, the years in which Lieutenant Espinoza, who participated in the assassination operation, was a student there. In

1970 Montes was the first Spanish Jesuit to obtain Salvadoran citizenship.

Father Montes gradually concentrated his energies on the UCA, where he was dean of the Faculty of Human and Natural Sciences. Sensitive to the social conflict taking place around him, Montes decided that he could better respond to the needs of El Salvador from within the social sciences, and he became a student again, obtaining a doctorate in social anthropology from the Universidad Complutense in 1978. After returning to the UCA, Montes taught sociology and directed the sociology department from 1980 until his death. He was a member of the editorial boards of the *Estudios Centroamericanos* and other academic reviews at the UCA.

As the civil war continued throughout the 1980s, Father Montes devoted himself to the study of the problems and needs of the thousands of displaced persons in El Salvador. The volumes which he published each year concerning this question are considered works of great authority in the matter. On weekends he ministered to a parish in the suburbs of San Salvador, where many displaced persons came in search of refuge after having been driven from war-torn rural areas.

From 1985 onwards, Father Montes directed the UCA's Institute of Human Rights (IDHUCA) and was called upon increasingly to speak in international fora concerning human rights, refugees, and internally displaced persons. On various occasions he testified before the Congress of the United States and in November 1989 was awarded a human rights prize in Washington, D.C. Father Montes also twice visited Salvadoran refugees at camps in Honduras; these refugees, now having returned to the north of El Salvador, have named their· community in Meanguera, Morazon "Segundo Montes."

Amando López Quintana, s.j.   Born in Burgos, Spain, in 1936, Father López was sent to El Salvador by his superiors in 1953. He studied the humanities, philosophy, and theology in Quito, Dublin, Rome, and Strasburg.

Father López divided his activity as a professor between El Salvador and Nicaragua. From 1970 to 1972 he served as rector of the seminary of San José de la Montaña in San Salvador and taught philosophy at the UCA in 1973 and 1974. From 1975 to 1983 he worked in Nicaragua, first as rector of the Central American College of Managua and later as rector of the Jesuit University of Nicaragua, also known as the Central American University.

At the end of 1984 Father López returned to El Salvador. At the time of his death he was teaching philosophy and theology in the UCA and was coordinator of the chair of philosophy. Father López had only recently moved into the university Jesuit community, having lived until 1988 with Jesuit students in Antiguo Cuscatlán. He contributed frequently to the *Estudios Centroamericanos* and *The Latin American Review of Theology*.

Juan Ramón Moreno Pardo, s.j.   Born in Villatuerta, Navarra, in Spain in 1933, Father Moreno was sent to El Salvador in 1951 to complete his novitiate. He obtained two degrees: one in humanities at the Catholic University of Quito in 1955, the other in theology at the University of St. Louis, Missouri in 1965.

Father Moreno dedicated the first years of his professional life to the natural sciences. In 1958 he began to give classes in chemistry in the Jesuit college at Granada in Nicaragua.

In 1968 he was sent to Rome to study Ignatian spirituality, as he had been appointed to serve as a master of novices, and in 1970 was in fact charged with the training of young Jesuits. He taught natural sciences at the UCA in El Salvador from 1971 to 1974, also serving as rector of the Externado San José for several months.

Father Moreno returned to Rome in 1974, where he remained until 1976, at which point he was sent to Panama. There he founded the Ignatian Center of Central America (Centro Ignaciano de Centroamérica) through which he promoted the spiritual teachings of the founder of the Jesuit order, Ignatius of Loyola. In 1980 he moved the Center to Nicaragua, and dedicated himself increasingly to theology and spirituality.

In 1985 Father Moreno was sent to El Salvador. At the UCA he served as Assistant Director of the Msgr. Romero Center of Theology, where the assassinations took place. He organized and automated the theological library of the Center, the best in San Salvador, and worked as secretary to the provincial, charged with maintaining the archives of the province. Sundays he provided pastoral assistance at a church run by the Jesuits in Santa Tecla.

Joaquín López y López, s.j. Father López y López was of a different generation than the other murdered priests and was the only one of them born in El Salvador.

Father López was born in 1918 to a well-to-do family. He entered the Society of Jesus in 1938 and did his novitiate in the United States, since at that time no center existed in Central America for the training of Jesuits. Later he studied in the Jesuit seminary at Oña, Spain.

Father López worked his whole life in El Salvador, dividing his time between the Externado San José and Fe y Alegría (Faith and Happiness), a Latin American scholastic extension program, which he initiated in 1969. Fe y Alegría assisted some 48,000 children, teenagers, and adults in thirty educational centers in El Salvador.

Father López did not work at the UCA, but was one of its founders and was an integral member of the Jesuit community at the University. In 1964 he led the campaign aimed at securing approval by the legislative assembly for the private universities law.

Julia Elba Ramos and **Celina Mariset Ramos.** Elba Ramos, the cook at a Jesuit student house near the UCA, and her 15-year-old daughter Celina were murdered, according to the statements of the lieutenants, because Col. Benavides "did not want any witnesses." The women lived with their husband and father in a small house near the site of the assassination and had sought refuge in the Jesuit residence. They had been sleeping at the residence since November 12th, but they had not been there the night the place was searched, and on the day of the assassination the soldiers were surprised to find them there.

Elba was born in Santiago de María in 1947. She met her husband at the end of the 1960s. Her first two children died at birth, the third—her daughter Celina—was born February 21, 1973, and she gave birth to a fourth child in 1976.

Elba began to work with the Jesuits as a cook and housekeeper in 1985. In June 1989 the family moved to the UCA campus, where her husband worked as a gardener and watchman and together with Father Montes took care of the flowers, vegetables, and fruit trees that surrounded the residence. At the time of her death, Celina was studying commerce at a secondary school.

Obdulio, Elba's husband, still tends the garden surrounding the Jesuit residence. The site of the assassination is now a rose garden, in which he has planted a red rose for each of the Jesuits and two yellow roses for his wife and daughter.

Amando López Quintana, S.J.

Segundo Montes Mozo, S.J.

Juan Ramón Moreno Pardo, S.J.

Joaquín López y López, S.J.

Ignacio Ellacuría, S.J.

Ignacio Martín-Baró, S.J.

Celina Maricet Ramos

Elba Julia Ramos

Ricardo Clement López

Chapter II
THE EVENTS

The FMLN Offensive

Shortly after 8:00 P.M. on the night of November 11, 1989, the FMLN launched the most powerful urban offensive in ten years of civil war in El Salvador, simultaneously attacking diverse points in the capital. In a matter of minutes, heavy combat could be heard in various places throughout the city. It is estimated that between 1,500 and 3,000 guerrilla fighters had entered San Salvador during the previous week. The troops appeared to be well prepared and capable of reprovisioning themselves with both ammunition and food. The working-class neighborhoods, which formed a ring around the city, were quickly transformed into rebel strongholds, occupied and controlled by the FMLN.

The Armed Forces clearly were not prepared to resist the strength of the attacks by the FMLN, nor to confront the guerrillas' ability to hold large sectors of the capital for several days. Some members of the Salvadoran military, as well as various civilian and diplomatic sources, describe the army as being a very disorganized institution during the first days of the FMLN offensive: it was caught by surprise and reacted poorly. Colonel René Emilio Ponce, at that time Chief of the Joint Military Command, and other high-ranking officers were interviewed as saying that the military seriously considered the possibility of their losing power or of San Salvador becoming a divided capital, like Beirut.

Death Threats Broadcast on the Radio

During the first hours of the fighting, Salvadoran radio stations provided excellent coverage of the FMLN offensive. Journalists as well as individual inhabitants of the city called the stations by telephone from areas where the combat was raging to report on the battles. However, at approximately 11:00 P.M. all of the stations received the order to merge as a national chain with Radio Cuscatlán, the Armed Forces channel.

Once under the control of the Armed Forces, the programming changed fundamentally. The nature of the telephone calls broadcasted also changed radically. The callers no longer requested information concerning the situation of their relatives nor sent messages to their families informing them that they were well. Instead, one caller after another denounced political personalities of the opposition, trade union leaders, members of the clergy, representatives of non-governmental organizations, etc., frequently terming them "front men for the FMLN." These declarations, vitriolic and vindictive in tone, generally incited the listeners to violence against the persons specified.

Continuing a long history of threats against the Society of Jesus, some of these attacks were directed at the Jesuits. Father Ellacuría was mentioned prominently by many of the persons who telephoned. "Ellacuría is a guerrilla. His head should be cut off," said one caller. "We should get Ellacuría and spit on him to death," said another. The Vice-President of the Republic, Francisco Merino, accused Ellacuría of "poisoning the minds" of Salvadoran youth at the UCA and in the Externado San José.

The Commandos of the Atlacatl Battalion Arrive in San Salvador

On the afternoon of November 13th, the military high command decided to create a special Security Command in an area which included the neighborhood around the UCA. Located only a few blocks away from the University were the headquarters of the military high command, the Ministry of Defense, the Military Academy, the National Intelligence Office (Dirección Nacional de Inteligencia–DNI), the San Benito battalion of the National Police, and two residential neighborhoods reserved for military personnel: the suburbs of Arce and Palermo. The command for the security zone was stationed at the Military Academy and placed under the direction of the Academy's director, Colonel Guillermo Alfredo Benavides.

By Monday it was clear that the guerrillas would not be dislodged easily. A curfew had been imposed from six in the evening until six in the morning. For the Armed Forces it was of capital importance that they protect their key centers of control. It was precisely in this area that the UCA was situated.

Given that the Military Academy normally does not maintain combat-ready troops, sections of other units were detailed to the Academy during the first days of the offensive. Among the troops assigned temporarily to the school was a commando unit of 47 men from the Atlacatl Battalion, an elite force established in 1981 and trained by the United States.[2] On November 10th, one day before the FMLN launched its offensive, thirteen members of the U.S. Special Forces from Fort Bragg in North Carolina began a training course at the barracks of the Atlacatl Battalion in Sitio del Niño. Among the trainees were members of the Atlacatl, seven of whom were indicted for the murder of the Jesuits.

Upon arriving in the capital, the commandos of the Atlacatl Battalion reported to the Military Academy to receive their orders. The lieutenants who were in charge of the unit reported directly to the military high command, where they were ordered to undertake a search at the residence of the Jesuits (see below). The fact that the commandos searched the house only two hours after having arrived in the capital suggests that the unit could have been brought to San Salvador principally for this purpose. Colonel Joaquín Arnoldo Cerna Flores, Chief of C-3 (Operations), declared in court on September 21, 1990 that he and Col. Ponce decided it was "appropriate" to send commandos to carry out the search, given their "age and combat experience, and because at this moment they had no other assigned mission."

The Search of the Jesuits' Residence

At six-thirty in the evening, a half hour after the curfew had begun, some 135 men surrounded the UCA campus in order to search the residence of the Jesuits there as well as the Center for Theolog-

---

[2] At least some of the members of the Atlacatl who came to the capital participated in the search of the Jesuits' residence on November 13, 1989.

ical Reflection, which was housed in the same building. A large number of the group entered the University grounds after having broken the lock on the rear gate which faces Cantábrico Road.

Father Ellacuría asked the officer in charge to identify himself, which he refused to do. Ellacuría, however, introduced himself, and the officer then approached Father Montes and Father Martín-Baró and demanded their names. It would later be learned that Lieutenant José Ricardo Espinoza Guerra, the officer in charge of the search, had been a student at the Jesuit secondary school Externado San José when Father Montes was its rector, but the latter did not recognize him. Ellacuría questioned the right of the army to search the building, which, he said, belonged to the Society of Jesus and not to the University. He asked to be allowed to call the Minister of Defense. The officer responded that in accordance with the state of siege declared the previous day, the soldiers could do whatever they wanted, and he added that they had orders to search the entire campus. Ellacuría suggested that they return the next day to search the rest of the UCA, but they did not return. Later Segundo Montes told friends that the troops belonged to the Atlacatl.

The Jesuits described the search as "correct" and said that the soldiers behaved well. Martín-Baró observed that the officer in charge "at all times addressed the professors respectfully." In previous inspections, the soldiers had stayed for hours, examining written materials to determine if they were "subversive." This time they posed no questions and did not seem interested in books or papers. Nothing led the Jesuits to believe that this intrusion was anything more than a routine search.[3]

THE NIGHT OF MURDER

The Preparations

At 11:00 P.M. on the night of November 15th, Lt. Espinoza was ordered to present himself to Col. Benavides at the Military

---

[3] See Martín-Baró, "Cateo a la Universidad Centroamericana y la communidad universitaria jesuítica," November 14, 1989. Father Ellacuría asked Martín-Baró to write up a small description of the search, which later was found in his computer following his death.

Academy.[4] There he met with Lieutenant Yusshy René Mendoza Vallecillos, who repeated that the colonel wished to see both him and Second-Lieutenant Gonzalo Guevara Cerritos. According to Espinoza's statement, once they were in his office, Col. Benavides said to them, "This is a situation where it is either them or us. We are going to start with the ringleaders. In our sector we hold the University, and Ellacuría is there." He turned immediately to Espinoza and continued, "You undertook the search and your people know the place. Use the same tactics as on the day of the search. You have to eliminate him. And I don't want any witnesses. Lieutenant Mendoza will go with you as the person in charge of the operation so that there won't be any problems."

Second-Lieutenant Guevara agrees with Espinoza but in addition puts the following words in the mouth of the colonel: "It has been the intellectuals who have directed the guerrilla war for a long time."

Later, before leaving the Military Academy, Espinoza asked Yusshy Mendoza for a camouflage bar with which to paint his face.

In all of the extrajudicial declarations one finds discrepancies between the version of Espinoza and that of Mendoza, especially with regard to who was in command of the operation.

When they were ready to go, Lt. Mendoza offered an AK-47 rifle[5] to whoever knew how to handle it. Oscar Mariano Amaya Grimaldi (nicknamed "Pilijay"), a soldier from the Atlacatl Battalion, responded that he knew how to work one, and the gun was given to him, but he does not remember which of the two lieutenants (Espinoza or Mendoza) handed it to him, since they were standing together. But he does remember having received information from Lt. Espinoza that they were going to kill "some criminal terrorists who are inside the UCA campus."

All agree that shortly after having received the order from Col. Benavides, they left the Military Academy in two Ford 250 pick-up trucks, accompanied by a group of approximately fif-

---

[4] The cited remarks and dialogues given in quotation marks are taken directly from the extrajudicial declarations and confessions.

[5] A rifle used by the fighters of the FMLN and not by the army. This involved a manoeuvre to blame the crime on the FMLN.

teen soldiers. They arrived at a cluster of several abandoned, half-constructed apartment buildings located on the western side of the UCA, and regrouped.

Here again discrepancies arise in the testimonies. In the end, however, it can be deduced that the three lieutenants gave instructions concerning the operation that they were about to undertake, and that all three knew what they were doing and collaborated in the execution of the plan, which naturally included an element of cover and security for the ones who were going to kill the priests. They decided who specifically was going to carry out the crime, and then the whole group marched in a column toward the UCA. At least 80 soldiers participated in the operation, although not all of them took a direct part in the killings. Before leaving the abandoned buildings, Amaya Grimaldi remembers that Lt. Mendoza said to him, "You are the key man."

Amaya Grimaldi understood by this "that he was the one who would be charged with killing the persons who were in that place." On the way, walking next to Lieutenants Espinoza and Mendoza, Pilijay heard the former say, referring to the AK-47 rifle, "Hide that shit."

At the UCA

They entered the UCA by the gate for pedestrians and waited for a moment next to the parking lot. In front of the lot the soldiers simulated a first attack, damaging the automobiles parked there and launching a grenade. The operation then unfolded in the form of three concentric circles. One group of soldiers remained in areas some distance away from the Msgr. Romero Center. Others surrounded the building, some of these climbing onto the roofs of nearby houses. Finally, a smaller, "select" group participated directly in the assassinations. Only the members of this group have been brought before the court.

With the house surrounded, the soldiers began to pound on the doors. At the same time, they broke into the lower floor of the building housing the Msgr. Romero Center of Theology, destroying and burning everything they found there. The soldiers surrounding the house of the Jesuits shouted to them to open the doors. Oscar Amaya ("Pilijay") remembers having said, "Let's see when they come out of there. According to you, I've got time to wait for them." Then he saw someone (Father Ellacuría) who said, "Wait, I'm going to open for you, but don't make such a disorder."

Ramiro Avalos Vargas, a sub-sergeant in the Atlacatl Battalion, testified that a soldier was pounding on the door with a thick piece of wood, that "after ten minutes of this pounding, a fair-haired man dressed in pajamas opened the door, which they had been striking with a thick trunk of wood, and told them not to continue banging on the door and the windows." This priest (Segundo Montes) was taken out onto the lawn in front of the residence, where Fathers Amando López, Ellacuría, Martín-Baró, and Juan Ramón Moreno were already gathered.

Tomás Zarpate Castillo, also a sub-sergeant in the Atlacatl, was guarding the door of the room in which Elba and Celina Ramos were being held at the order of the "lieutenant of the Military Academy," as Yusshy Mendoza was called by all those who filed declarations.

Antonio Ramiro Avalos and Oscar Amaya say they ordered the Jesuits to lie down on the grass while they remained alone with them "for fear of losing control of the situation." Meanwhile the search of the house continued, where Father Joaquín López y López had managed to hide in one of the rooms.

The Assassinations

Ramiro Avalos says that Lt. Espinoza, with Lt. Mendoza by his side, called to him and asked, "When are you going to proceed?" The sub-sergeant declares that he understood this phrase "as an order to eliminate the men who were lying face down." Amaya came nearer and said, "Let's do it." And then the shooting started. Avalos Vargas assassinated Fathers Ramón Moreno and Amando López. Amaya Grimaldi killed Fathers Ellacuría, Martín-Baró, and Montes. Espinoza and Mendoza remained at a distance of ten meters, according to the statements of the two executioners.

While this was occurring, Sub-Sergeant Tomás Zarpate "was

providing security" (according to his own declarations) and keeping Elba and Celina locked in a room. Upon hearing a voice give the order "Now!" and then the shots that followed, "he also fired at the two women" until he was sure that they were dead, because "they were no longer moaning."

At this moment, when the shooting stopped, Father Joaquín López appeared in the doorway of the residence. The soldiers called to him and Pilijay said that he answered, "You are not going to kill me because I don't belong to any organization." He then went back in the house. The version of Corporal Angel Pérez Vásquez of the Atlacatl Battalion concurs in part with the preceding account: Father Joaquín López came out of his hiding place upon hearing the shots, saw the bodies and immediately went back into the house. The soldiers said to him, "Father, come here." But, the account continues: "The gentleman didn't pay any notice, and when he was going to enter one of the rooms, there was a soldier there who shot him." Pérez Vásquez continues his narrative by saying that when Father López fell into the room, the soldier approached to inspect the place." And as he stepped over the man who had been shot, he felt him grab at his feet, at which he stepped back and shot him a further four times."

The crime having been completed, a flare was launched. This was the signal for the troops to withdraw. As some of the soldiers did not move, a second flare was fired. With the retreat underway, Avalos Vargas, nicknamed "Satan" by his friends, was passing by the room in which Elba and Celina were shot, when he heard someone gasping for breath. He immediately realized that the victims were only wounded and would have to be shot again. "Lighting a match, and observing that inside the room the two women who had been shot were straining in each others arms and struggling for breath, he ordered a soldier by the name of Sierra Ascencio to finish them off." Jorge Alberto Sierra Ascencio, a soldier in the Atlacatl Battalion, "fired a burst of around ten bullets at the bodies of the two women until they stopped moving," remembers Avalos. When Sierra Asencio realized that the investigation was beginning to point toward his group, he deserted.

There was nothing left now. Amaya Grimaldi heard Espinoza

Guerra give the following order to Cpl. Cotta Hernández: "Put them inside, even though they're scoundrels." Then Cpl. Cotta dragged the body of Father Juan Ramón Moreno to the second room of the residence and dumped it there. When he went back out, Cotta realized that all the others had left, and he did the same, leaving the other bodies on the lawn.

An hour had passed since they had entered the campus and faked a battle at the parking lot near the university chapel. Cerritos fired the second flare. Pilijay, meanwhile, had a beer in the kitchen at the scene of the crime.

Destruction of the Center of Theology

As they left, the soldiers staged a mock attack on the Msgr. Romero Center of Theology. It was part of the plan. Colonel Benavides' record of operations reads: "[A]t zero hours and thirty minutes on the sixteenth, criminal terrorists firing grenade launchers damaged the Theology building at the studies center; no casualties reported."

On doors and walls in the ground floor of the Msgr. Romero Center, the soldiers wrote the acronym FMLN. As they left, one of them wrote on a board, "The FMLN has executed some spies of the enemy. Victory or death! FMLN." A graphological analysis later demonstrated that the handwriting of 2nd. Lt. Guevara Cerritos and that of Sub-Sgt. Avalos Vargas both "presented characteristics similar to" the writing on the board. Either of the two could have been the author.

The Msgr. Romero Center of Theology was set on fire from inside. Afterwards, an M-60 machine gun was set up, which had been brought from the Military Academy, and they began shooting at the building that housed the Center. Pilijay, who had finished his beer, arrived in time to fire a Low anti-tank rocket, which exploded against the iron gate in the corridor to the priests' residence. Other soldiers also fired and one of them launched two M-79 grenades against the building. Neither Cotta Hernández, who collaborated by dragging away the body of Father Juan Ramón Moreno, nor the sergeant nicknamed "Savage" and his patrol, who fired against the building, nor the soldiers who entered the Msgr. Romero Center and burned and sacked its contents, were ever brought to trial. The testimony of Lt. Yusshy Mendoza contains a final recollection from the scene of the crime. "An unknown soldier carried off a light, coffee-colored satchel." The five thousand dollars of the Alfonso Comín Prize, awarded to Father Ellacuría a few days before, disappeared into the darkness.

THE ACCUSED

Colonel Guillermo Alfredo Benavides Moreno. Colonel Benavides, 46 years old, is the first high-ranking officer to have been prosecuted for a crime against human rights in El Salvador. Benavides is a member of the *Tandona*, the class that graduated from the Military Academy in 1966, a class which includes the most powerful officers in the Armed Forces.

Benavides began his military career in the air force. As a lieutenant colonel in 1984, he was named commander of the Belloso Battalion and, later, commandant of Military Detachment No. 3 in La Unión. In 1987 he was appointed head of Military Detachment No. 5 in Cojutepeque, the following year as chief of the Intelligence Unit (C-2) of the Joint Military Command. He remained in this latter post for a year before being named director of the Military Academy "Capitán General Gerardo Barrios" on June 1, 1989.

As director of the strategically placed Military Academy, during the FMLN offensive on November 13, 1989, Col. Benavides was named head of the Security Command, which included within its perimeters the most important military installations in the country as well as the UCA. Troops from several different military units were placed under his operational command, including soldiers of the Atlacatl Battalion.

Colonel Benavides was accused of murder, acts of terrorism, acts in preparation of terrorism, and inciting and conspiring to commit acts of terrorism. He has never confessed to having played even the slightest role in the killings and professes total ignorance of such a mission (including the search of November 13th) being carried out by the commandos of the Atlacatl at the UCA, despite the fact that these were under his command. According to the rules of the army, only he could have given the order authorizing the deployment of troops and the use of weaponry from the Military Academy, including the AK-47 rifle and the M-60 machine gun. Furthermore, he is accused in the testimony of Lt. Espinoza and 2nd. Lt. Guevara Cerritos, who say they received from Benavides himself together with Lt. Mendoza the order to kill the Jesuits and to leave no witnesses.

Lieutenant José Ricardo Espinoza Guerra. Lieutenant Espinoza, 30 years of age, studied at the Externado San José until 1979, during the time that Father Segundo Montes was rector of the school. He graduated from the Military Academy in 1984 and, like Col. Benavides, began his military career in the air force. After three years in the air force he was expelled on January 30, 1987, for "serious errors committed during service." He was immediately reassigned to the Atlacatl Battalion.

Espinoza was sent to the United States on various occasions: he studied English at Oakland Air Force Base in San Antonio, Texas, from March 5 to August 9, 1985; he also received training as a pilot there from August 19 to September 22 of the same year, remaining at the base until December 31st. Authorized to participate in a further, unspecified official mission to the United States from January 1 to November 25, 1986, he returned again to the U.S. in 1988 to follow an officers' course given by the Special Forces.

Espinoza, known as "the Bull," was accused of assassination, acts of terrorism, acts in preparation of terrorism, and inciting and conspiring to commit acts of terrorism. The principle proof against Espinoza is his own extrajudicial confession, recorded by the CIHD January 13, 1990. He was the direct commander of the troops implicated in the assassination.

Espinoza's extrajudicial confession constitutes the most complete narrative account of the events surrounding the crime. He tells of having received the order from Col. Benavides to eliminate Father Ellacuría and not to leave any witnesses. With Espinoza's agreement, Benavides assigned Lt. Yusshy Mendoza, from the Military Academy, as head of the operation "to ensure that there are no problems." Espinoza describes how he transported his troops and concentrated three patrols already located in this area around the UCA. Nevertheless, inside the campus Espinoza says he distanced himself from the action and went away from the residence of the Jesuits with tears in his eyes. His troops, however, place him closer to the scene and describe him as having ordered the soldiers who were holding the five Jesuits face down on the lawn to "proceed." He claims that he protested later to Benavides about what had happened, but that the latter reassured him, saying, "Calm down, don't worry about it. You have my support, believe me."

Lieutenant Yusshy René Mendoza Vallecillos. Lieutenant Mendoza, 27 years old, graduated from the Military Academy with Espinoza Guerra in 1984 and was assigned to the Artillery Brigade. On September 1, 1987, he was appointed to the Military Academy as chief of section. Mendoza accompanied Espinoza in the OCS course given at the Army Infantry School at Ft. Benning in the United States at the beginning of 1982. In 1988 he returned to Ft. Benning to participate in a commando course.

Mendoza was accused of murder, acts of terrorism, acts in preparation of terrorism, inciting and conspiring to commit terrorism, and actual concealment of evidence, this last charge for his role in burning the register of troop movements to and from the Academy. Though Mendoza, like Espinoza, denies any direct participation in the killings, he provided the principal proof against himself in his extrajudicial confession. Others among the accused attribute to him an active role, that of having been in command of the operation, having handed over the AK-47 rifle to Pvt. Amaya, and having given the orders. While Mendoza later denied having made the statements contained in his extrajudicial confession, he did admit to his role in burning the register of movements to and from the Military Academy, though he says that he did so on the orders of the acting subdirector of the school, Lt. Col. Camilo Hernández.

Second Lieutenant Gonzalo Guevara Cerritos. Second Lieutenant Guevara Cerritos, 28 years of age, entered the army in 1980 but did not attend the Military Academy, rising through the ranks instead on his own merits. He was promoted to the rank of Second Lieutenant at the end of 1988. He began this career in the air force, then served in the Belloso Rapid Reaction Battalion from 1982 to 1988; subsequently he moved to the Atlacatl as a section commander. From July to December 1988 he was in the United States to receive OCS training at Ft. Benning, Georgia. At the time of the assassinations he was the executive officer of an Atlacatl commando unit.

Guevara Cerritos ("Wild Cat") faced charges of murder, acts of terrorism, acts in preparation of terrorism, and inciting and conspiring to commit acts of terrorism. Like the two lieutenants, in his extrajudicial confession he denied any direct participation in the assassinations but admitted having taken part in the operation at the UCA on the night of the crime. His confession constitutes the most important proof against him. There he admits having been present when Col. Benavides gave the order to go to the UCA and carry out the operation to eliminate the Jesuits. In his statement before the court, he calculated that some 80 soldiers from the Atlacatl participated in the operation.

Sub-Sergeant Ramiro Avalos Vargas. Sub-Sergeant Avalos Vargas, 23 years old, is known as "The Toad" or "Satan." He directed the second commando patrol of the Atlacatl Battalion. Avalos Vargas received training in small-unit management in the United States from September 30 to December 14, 1988. He was accused of murder, acts of terrorism, and acts in preparation of terrorism. In his confession he admitted killing two of the priests (Father Amando López and Father Juan Ramón Moreno). Following instructions from Lt. Espinoza, Avalos Vargas gave the order to Amaya Grimaldi, who was also guarding the priests, "Let's get on with it." As he was leaving the residence after having shot the Jesuits, he heard the sound of groaning coming from one of the rooms and went to check on it. When he saw the two women wounded on the floor, clinging to each other and moaning, he ordered Pvt. Jorge Alberto Sierra Ascencio to shoot them dead, which he did.

Sub-Sergeant Tomás Zarpate Castillo. Sub-Sergeant Zarpate Castillo, 30 years of age and known as "Samson," was chief of the third commando patrol in the Atlacatl. He was accused of murder, acts of terrorism, and acts in preparation of terrorism.

Like the other members of the troop, he admitted his role in the crime. Specifically, in his extrajudicial declaration he admitted having shot the two women and leaving them for dead.

Corporal Angel Pérez Vásquez. Corporal Pérez Vásquez, 31 years old, was a member of the fourth commando patrol. Like Sub-Sgt. Avalos Vargas, he was sent to the United States in 1987 for a course in small-unit management. In his extrajudicial declaration he admitted having fired four shots, killing Father López y López when the priest, lying on the ground after having been wounded by another soldier, began clutching at his feet. He was accused of murder, acts of terrorism, and acts in preparation of terrorism.

Private Oscar Mariano Amaya Grimaldi. Private Amaya Grimaldi, 28 years of age and known as "Pilijay," entered the Atlacatl Battalion in 1982. He had been in a commando unit for 18 months and knew how to use an AK-47 rifle. In his extrajudicial confession, Amaya Grimaldi admitted that he had been given an AK-47 by Lt. Mendoza (or by Lt. Espinoza, he "doesn't remember which, because the two were standing together"). Mendoza told him afterwards that he was "the key man." Amaya Grimaldi admitted that with this rifle he fired various shots at Fathers Ellacuría, Martín-Baró, and Montes, and that later he also fired at Fathers Amando López and Juan Ramón Moreno, who had already been shot by Avalos Vargas. After the killings, he says, he drank a beer in the kitchen of the residence before joining the fusillade against the building. He was accused of murder, acts of terrorism, and acts in preparation of terrorism.

Private Jorge Sierra Ascencio. Private Sierra Ascencio, 28 years old, entered the Atlacatl in July 1985 and the commando unit in 1987. A member of the second patrol, commanded by Avalos Vargas, he deserted and fled in 1989, and as a result made no extrajudicial or judicial declaration. He was judged in absentia. Sierra Ascencio was accused of murder, since it was he who, obeying an order from Sub-Sgt. Avalos, shot dead the two women, who were already wounded.

Colonel Guillermo Alfredo Benavides Moreno

The judge; the accused

Chapter III

THE TRIAL

As in other Latin American countries, the Salvadoran system of criminal procedure establishes two stages for the adjudication of a criminal case: the *sumario,* or investigative phase, in which prima-facie evidence is gathered for the existence of the crime and the possible responsibility or innocence of suspects, and the *plenario,* or trial stage in the strict sense of the term, in which the judge, if he does not dismiss the case for lack of evidence, will ultimately decree the conviction or acquittal of the accused. But in contrast to what occurs in other countries, in El Salvador the judge charged with the indictment proceeding (*sumario*) is the same judge who is responsible for directing the judicial hearing (*plenario*). In the opinion of the ICJ observer, this is not a good solution, as it does not create the best conditions for the Defense or for the Office of the Public Prosecutor to obtain, for example, access to specific evidence denied them during the *sumario* phase. Indeed, there is very little probability of obtaining the realization of specific elements of an investigation when it is necessary to request this of the same magistrate who previously refused such a request because he did not deem these elements to be pertinent.

THE INVESTIGATIVE AND INDICTMENT PHASE *(Sumario)*

Immediately after the crime had been committed, as is required by Salvadoran law, Justice of the Peace No. 3 undertook the first steps of the investigation by examining and identifying the site of the crime and the bodies of the victims, and gathering possible evidence. A second examination was later undertaken which included the participation, together with the Justice of the Peace, of both Criminal Judge No. 4, Dr. Ricardo Zamora, who would be charged with conducting the process, and the representative of the Public Prosecutor's Office. It should be noted that neither of these inspections turned up any arms or documentation from the FMLN.

Over the course of the following days, various specific steps of the investigation were carried out, including the interrogation of neighbors who could have heard or seen something, the forensic examination of the bodies to determine the precise wounds inflicted and the cause of death, as well as the time at which the deaths occurred (the hour was established as 2:30 A.M. on November 16th).

As soon as the crime was discovered, and in view of its particular repercussions, President Cristiani himself entrusted the inquiry to the Commission for the Investigation of Criminal Acts (Comisión de Investigación de Hechos Delictivos—CIHD). This is a special body created in 1985 with funds from the U.S. Agency for International Development (AID), a United States governmental organization. Its initial responsibility was that of investigating cases of human rights violations in which members of the Armed Forces were implicated. Its directors are themselves members of the Armed Forces, and the detectives that make up the body, though they belong to the National Police, are subject to military statutes and thus to military discipline and the hierarchical chain of command. Under such conditions it was hardly likely that this Commission would investigate thoroughly the responsibility of military personnel in the actions at the UCA. Moreover, experience has demonstrated that there have been practically no cases in which the CIHD had established the responsibility of military personnel in acts violating human rights.

Once again this Commission did not adequately accomplish its work, allowing evidence to be lost, giving the principal suspects time to formulate their alibis, and failing to promptly carry out a number of investigative steps normal in criminal cases. Only several months later did it undertake laboratory analyses and ballistics tests enabling it to establish the types of weapons used. To give an idea of the magnitude of the military operation undertaken on the night of the crime, it is sufficient to note that around 200 spent rifle cartridges were found in the area, fired both during the assassinations as well as in the destruction of the Msgr. Romero Center of Theology.

In short, nothing concrete emerged from the activity of the CIHD until the guilty persons began to be uncovered through other channels. It was only at this point that the conduct of the investigation became more positive.

At first, high-ranking military officers and politicians attributed responsibility for the killings to the FMLN, one even going so far as to say that this was a tactic used by the Front to cast blame on the Armed Forces for a crime that the guerrillas themselves had committed (Col. Heriberto Hernández, Chief of the Treasury Police; declaration recorded 9/Dec/1989.) The Minister of Foreign Relations also qualified the crime as "an act of desperation by the Left." The police investigators being subject to the military hierarchical chain, it was highly improbable that they would attempt to advance farther or in contradiction to what their own chiefs were affirming.

But the versions pinning blame on the FMLN very quickly proved to be groundless. The killings had provoked a wave of indignation, not only inside the country but also abroad. The Archbishop of San Salvador, Msgr. Rivera, stated in his sermon of November 19, 1989 that he had a strong suspicion that the authors of the crime were elements of the Armed Forces. Statements condemning the action followed quickly one upon the other. In the United States various members of Congress affirmed that if the assassins were not brought to justice, Congress would review the assistance which it was providing to El Salvador.[6]

All of this worked to change the perspective of the authorities. President Cristiani officially requested the collaboration of the FBI, Scotland Yard, and the Canadian and Spanish police forces to advise the CIHD.

The Truth Begins to Appear

The Armed Forces are not an "auxiliary organ of the law" (art. 11, Code of Criminal Procedure, October 1973) and do

---

[6] In the last ten years, El Salvador has been the country in the region which has received the most military assistance from the United States, amounting to several billion dollars.

not have powers of investigation in criminal cases. Nevertheless, on January 5, 1990 the Ministry of Defense unexpectedly set up a so-called Commission of Honor of the Armed Forces (Comisión de Honor de la Fuerza Armada), composed of six senior officers of the military and two civilian lawyers charged with clarifying the facts of the case. And then, proceeding in an inexplicable manner and using methods that have no basis in judicial procedure, they came up with nine culprits.

The climate created by the events may have forced the high military authorities, who required continued military assistance from the United States, to bring at least some of those responsible to trial. In any case, what the police investigations had not been able to achieve in two months was accomplished in a matter of days by the Commission of Honor, which informed President Cristiani on January 12th that it had the names of the nine guilty persons. The following day, the President publicly announced the names. It was on the basis of these developments that the investigation limited itself to rising as far as Col. Benavides. The CIHD made no effort to determine whether anyone higher in the chain of command was also responsible. One of the objectives of the Commission of Honor seems also to have been that of avoiding compromising the army as an institution, specifically by reducing responsibility for the deed to the officer who gave the order and to the unit that executed it. In limiting the investigation, the results of the trial were also already being limited.

There was a background to this "revelation": a few days before, an officer of the U.S. Army, Major Eric Buckland, who had been carrying out an advisory mission to the Joint High Command of the Salvadoran Armed Forces and who had returned to his country, informed his superiors that on the basis of something confided to him by a Salvadoran colonel named Carlos Avilés, he had learned that Col. Benavides had admitted his participation in the murder of the Jesuits to Lieutenant Colonel Manuel A. Rivas, Chief of the CIHD. And the CIHD had not said a word about it. After asserting this, Major Buckland repeated his declarations to the FBI on numerous occasions, but ended by retracting his statements, explaining that the FBI agents had confused him and "put pressure on me. . . .

I could feel that they were trying to pressure me in Washington." Although his testimony was ruled invalid, and in addition he was a witness who had not directly seen the events (but had only been told about them), his declarations nevertheless were important for unblocking the investigation.

Before the names of the presumed culprits were made known publicly, the CIHD arrested eight of the accused, while the ninth, Private Jorge Alberto Sierra Ascencio, deserted his unit and fled. He would later be judged in absentia, as is authorized by Salvadoran law.

The eight military men arrested made declarations to the police (CIHD). With the exception of Col. Benavides, who always denied having participated or even having given orders to carry out the operation, all of the others, without coercion or pressure (this was later confirmed before the judge by two eyewitnesses to the declarations), *confessed extensively, precisely, and in detail concerning their participation.* Four of the seven (all members of the troop) had directly carried out the killings.

These declarations were truthful and consistent. They recounted in exact detail the departure of the troops from the Military Academy where they were quartered, the instructions they received, when they received them and from whom, the weapons they carried, the route they took to the UCA, the manner in which they entered the campus and the residence of the Jesuits; the specific role played by each one of them, the precise hour in which the events took place, how they assassinated the priests, in which spot and with which arms, who specifically killed whom, and what they did with the bodies; how and from where they fired their weapons against the Center of Theology, largely destroying it; how a total of 80 men from their own Atlacatl Battalion, without directly taking part in the assassinations, had participated in the operation, performing functions of support, security, lookout, etc. In short, the declarations were complete, precise, and consistent with one another, with the exception of those of the three officers (two lieutenants and a second-lieutenant). The confessions of the three officers contradict one another in minor ways concerning specific aspects such as who was in charge of the operation, and each of them tried to minimize the level of his own participation. But they admit having taken part in the entire operation and having received orders and instructions directly from the colonel. And there is not the slightest discrepancy among the statements of the other troop members.

Shortly thereafter they began to be interrogated within the framework of the judicial process by Judge Zamora (judge No. 4 of the criminal division). At first various of the accused declined to make statements, claiming to be ill or confused. When they finally did make their declarations, all of them maintained their innocence, going so far as to deny even having been at the UCA and refuting what they themselves had affirmed in such detail and precision. They explained this radical shift in their position by claiming simply that they had been "intimidated" and "forced" into making their original confessions by agents of the CIHD.

In the Salvadoran system this type of declaration is known as an "extrajudicial confession," that is to say, one made to the police rather than before a tribunal. In order for the statement to be accepted as valid, the procedural law requires that two witnesses who were present at the confession and listened to it declare before the judge that they indeed witnessed and heard the confession being given, that it was made freely, and that the person to whom it is attributed "was not the object of physical force or intimidation" (art. 496 of the Code of Criminal Procedure). In such cases "the extrajudicial confession" remains juridically validated and will be considered as "sufficient proof," provided that "said confession is in concordance with other existing elements of the case in a trial concerning the same punishable offense" (the same art. 496).

In this case, the validation was done according to the law (the eyewitnesses confirmed the conditions) and the confessions of each of the accused tallied perfectly not only with all of the others (even to the smallest detail, being logical, coherent, and plausible), but also with other elements of the trial: the ballistic tests, the type of arms employed, the results of the autopsies concerning the direction from which the bullets were fired, etc.

Other legal systems require a confession to be repeated before the judge in order for it to be accepted as juridically valid, with statements made to the police through administrative channels being considered only as pieces of evidence. But in order to overturn such evidence and retract what was confessed to the police, the accused must explain reasonably and adequately why he confessed to something which he now says is false. Furthermore, the confession is only one of the measures of proof—even if a very important one—which the law recognizes and which are gathered with other measures. A person may be properly convicted—and this frequently happens—without having made a confession; similarly, someone who confesses to an offense may not be found guilty if his confession is not "in concordance with other existing elements in the trial." In short, the simple fact of having retracted a confession does not protect a person from criminal conviction.

On January 17, 1990, the judge decreed the provisional detention of the nine soldiers, accused for the moment of eight murders (art. 154 of the Criminal Code), deeming sufficient proof to have been found concerning their respective participation, including that of Col. Benavides, who had always denied his involvement. He also decreed the seizure of their possessions and property to cover the civil responsibility resulting from the offenses. At the same time, he ordered the capture of the only one of the accused not to have been detained, Pvt. Sierra Ascencio. Later, as will be seen, he also charged all of the men with crimes of terrorism.

The entire investigative proceedings comprising the summary stage were marked by limitations, omissions, reticence, and actions that cannot be clearly explained. One of these involves what happened to the testimony of a direct witness, Mrs. Lucía Barrera de Cerna, who worked as a cleaner at the UCA rectory and the Jesuit Provincial Curia. On November 15th, unable to return to her home in Soyapango, the site of intense combat, she telephoned Father Martín-Baró (one of the victims) to ask whether he could provide shelter for her, her husband, Jorge Cerna, and her small daughter. Father Martín-Baró offered them a room in the former Jesuit residence, located in a street lateral to the scene of the murders (i.e., to the residence where the Jesuits were currently living) and about 30 meters away from the house. That night, upon hearing shots being fired sometime after 1:00 A.M., Mrs. de Cerna looked out of one of the windows facing the corridor of the Jesuits' residence and made out five men in camouflage uniforms and military caps firing their weapons at the house. She could see them, though the electricity supply had been interrupted that night, because it was full moon. She managed to hear Father Martín-Baró shout at them, "This is an injustice. You're completely rotten!" Later she heard more shots and explosions. Her husband also could see a group of soldiers from another window. She and her husband, together with four UCA watchmen who, frightened by the shooting, had remained shut in the small house next door, discovered the dead bodies at dawn on November 16th.

Mrs. de Cerna related her experience to the other Jesuits, who took her to the Spanish Embassy. There she made sworn declarations before the judge, the public prosecutor, and members of the CIHD. Transferred later to the French Embassy for reasons of security, she left in a French airplane for the United States, where she was received by Jesuits. There she and her husband were interrogated by the FBI. She later asserted that she was intimidated by the FBI to the point of changing her testimony and declaring that she saw nothing on the night of the crime. The ICJ observer finds it difficult to understand by what right FBI agents interrogated a witness about a crime committed in El Salvador.

Another negative aspect was that delays in action by the CIHD investigators permitted the written registers of troop movements to and from the Military Academy to be burned in December 1989. The registers most probably would have made it possible to establish the departure and return of the Atlacatl Battalion on the night of November 15–16, 1989. At the trial it was determined that all comings and goings at the school were recorded in such registers. As a result, the former sub-director of the Academy, Lieutenant Colonel Carlos Camilo Hernández, was criminally indicted for "destruction of evidence" for having ordered the burning of the registers. The judge will have to decide in a separate trial, which does not require the formation of a jury, whether the lieutenant colonel was guilty of "actual concealment" (art. 471 of the Criminal Code).

In general, in the CIHD investigations can be seen a lack of interest in arriving at the truth, a lamentable degree of negligence, and, above all, a desire to limit the investigation. As an example, we might cite the fact that various military officers who could have provided information concerning the movements of the Atlacatl Battalion on the night of the crime were not interrogated, or were questioned only months afterwards when "they did not remember having seen anything." The officer responsible for the zone in which the UCA was located, Col. Benavides, was interrogated a month and a half after the crime.

Another factor which conspired against the establishment of the truth, but which obviously is not attributable to the CIHD, is the disposition contained in art. 205 of the Code of Criminal Procedure which allows certain dignitaries of the state, including "the heads of the armed forces with a command rank of general or colonel" not to appear in person as witnesses in court but to provide their statement in writing by "sworn affidavit." Certain military chiefs took advantage of this exception to the rule on appearing personally; such was the case of Colonel René Ponce Torres, at that time Chief of the Joint Military Command. In his written response to the questions of the judge, he declared that on November 13, 1989 (the date of the search at the Jesuits' residence), he had authorized the entry of the soldiers because "terrorists had opened fire from within the UCA campus." At the trial, the falsity of this statement was demonstrated. By contrast, in an attempt to provide an example of collaboration with the judiciary, the President of the Republic did not make use of this exemption, and testified in person before the court.

In November 1990 Judge Zamora added other charges against the nine defendants: those of having committed "acts of terrorism" (art. 400 of the Criminal Code) and "acts in preparation of terrorism" (art. 402 CP). These nine indictments stemmed from the attack involving heavy weaponry against the Msgr. Romero Center of Theology; there the men of the Atlacatl used R-16 rifles, anti-tank rockets, and grenades, and also started a fire in the building. The resulting flames were of such intensity that several panes of glass melted, including that covering an oil painting of Msgr. Romero in the main hall (Msgr. Romero was assassinated in 1980, apparently by members of the Armed Forces, but the ensuing investigation, also directed by Judge Ricardo Zamora, never advanced). The new indictments caused considerable tension in the Armed Forces, which had never before been accused of terrorism and which considered terrorism as an offense that could only be imputed to the armed opposition. The four officers were also charged with the crime of "inciting and conspiring to commit acts of terrorism" (art. 403 PC). We will comment on this aspect of the indictment (three different offenses for the same criminal intention) later, in our evaluation of the trial.

On December 6, 1990, Criminal Judge No. 4 announced the termination of the *sumario,* or investigative phase of the case and the opening of the *plenario.* As mentioned above, with this phase began the trial in the strict sense of the term. The object of a trial is "to discuss differing views concerning the elements collected during the instruction, and to receive evidence . . . in order to establish the guilt or innocence of the accused and to pass a sentence accordingly" (art. 296 CPP). As also previously indicated, the judge in charge of the *plenario* will be the same judge that instructed the case in the *sumario,* a procedure which, in our opinion and for the reasons we have given, does not represent a good legal solution.

THE TRIAL PHASE *(Plenario)*

Confirmation of the Indictment

On December 19, 1990, the lawyers for the defense introduced a motion of appeal against the decision of the court to judge the accused for offenses of murder and terrorism (art. 298 of the Code of Criminal Procedure). In general, they maintained that there was insufficient proof, particularly against Col. Benavides, and that the evidence invoked by the judge was invalid because the confessions involved had been given more than 72 hours after the arrest of the suspects (art. 496, 1 of the CPP), and because in accordance with art. 499 CPP: "Persons who are co-authors or accomplices in the same crime or fault may not appear as witnesses against one another." Although this latter rule is encoded in the Salvadoran system, we cannot fail to point out that it seems a very curious one, since logically nobody knows the facts of a case better than someone who participated in them. We will return to this aspect later. Another argument of the defense was that the presiding judge was improper, because for territorial reasons the case should have been heard by the judge of Santa Tecla and not by one from San Salvador.

The judge maintained his interlocutory, refusing these objections (correctly, in our opinion). He held that with respect to the colonel there existed a personal conviction of guilt, in accordance with the rules of critical assessment (art. 499 CPP) admitted in the Code, but also in agreement with a number of mutually consistent pieces of evidence leading to the same conclusion. Regarding the other allegations, he stated that he had not taken into account the declarations of the defendants against each other, but rather their own extrajudicial confessions, juridically validated, as well as other pieces of testimony and gathered evidence, such as expert analyses, etc.

As a result of the appeal the case was submitted to a higher tribunal, the First Chamber of Criminal Law (Cámara Primera de lo Penal) of San Salvador. On April 9, 1991, this collegial body confirmed the decision of Judge Zamora in all its particulars. Using a series of weighty arguments, the Chamber agreed that all nine of the accused must share responsibility for shaping the assassinations, even if the colonel had not confessed. He was Chief of the Security Command and was able to give orders without consulting his superiors; but whoever gave orders outside the framework of legality was required to answer for such orders. The tribunal cited art. 8 of the Military Ordinance, which holds the commanding officer responsible for the orders which he gives. Although this aspect will be analyzed in more detail below, the ICJ observer wishes to point out here that a dangerous confusion can exist between two spheres of distinct responsibility: criminal and military. Criminal law does not admit objective responsibility according to a hierarchical system; such responsibility is always personal and subjective. If the colonel is guilty, as we believe he is, it is *for having given orders as the commanding officer,* but not simply by virtue of having been the commander. The tribunal also agreed with the charging of "acts of terrorism" and "acts in preparation of terrorism," based on the evidence collected concerning the attack perpetrated, the arms used, and what was recounted about the meeting held at the Military Academy on the night of November 15th. A passage from its ruling says that "the constitutional mission of the Armed Forces does not include the right to commit crimes." The Chamber affirmed, moreover, that the incriminating remarks made against one another by the accused had not been taken into account, but only their own freely given confessions. In conclusion, the tribunal rejected the defense lawyers' request for dismissal of the case. The lawyers for Col. Benavides and Lt. Espinoza then filed motions of *habeas corpus,* which were rejected by the Supreme Court of Justice on May 8th.

Meanwhile, with tensions caused by the trial running high, two of the specified prosecuting attorneys (i.e., prosecutors assigned to a particular case), attorneys Henry Campos and Sidney Blanco, resigned in January 1991 in protest against the attitude of their superior, the Attorney General of the Republic. According to them, he had ordered them to limit their cross-examination of military personnel convoked as witnesses at the trial, and prohibited them from continuing to prosecute other military men for the crime of false testimony.

In May, however, the two ex-prosecutors appeared before the judge in the capacity of "private accusers," representing the families of the victims and the UCA (art. 50 CPP) and constituting a civil party to the trial (i.e., demanding compensation from the accused for the damages caused; arts. 134 CP and 69 CPP). With the case now in the *plenario* stage, the private accusers requested a whole series of investigative steps and a search for evidence, but the judge accepted only a few of these. Nevertheless, as he did agree to make room for the declarations of witnesses living in the United States (military advisers who had been in El Salvador) through the "commissioned magistrate" system, the space allotted for evidence was widened.

Having gathered 28 files of documentation, containing thousands of pages, the judge decided to convoke the Public Trial.

Selection and Installation of a Jury of the People

The public trial forms part of the *plenario*, and specifically takes the shape of a hearing held in the presence of all the parties and the public. Due to the type of offenses with which the accused were charged, it was only fitting that the case be tried before a jury of the people. Such juries, composed of five citizens serving as representatives of Salvadoran society, are called upon to pronounce a verdict of innocence or guilt (arts 315 ff., CPP). Any Salvadoran may be called upon to take part in a jury, as long as he or she fulfills the qualifications required by law and is not himself/herself affected by some incompatibility or legal incapacity (art. 318 CPP).

The law establishes very precise and detailed procedures for selecting those citizens who compose the lists from which juries are drawn. Each tribunal makes up partial lists containing 15 names: when the moment comes for a trial, the judge, in the presence of the various parties, proceeds with what the law calls an *insaculación* (drawing from a sack), producing first a partial list of candidates and later conducting a drawing.

Once the date is fixed for the public trial, the persons whose names have been drawn are summoned (this includes more than the required five persons, in case some do not show up or are excused or rejected by one of the parties). Only at this moment is it made known on which case they have been called to participate. When a jury of five members has been constituted by the judge, a sixth person—the first alternate—is required to follow all of the debates, so as to be able to knowledgeably and informedly replace an official juror who cannot continue as the result of illness or another justifiable reason. During the entire period of the public hearing—which in very exceptional cases like the present one can last longer than one day—the jurors must remain sequestered.

Jury duty is obligatory, and anyone who fails to appear before the court after being summoned or who fails to discharge the duty after having been chosen to sit on a jury will be liable to a fine (art. 387 CCP), although the amount of the fine is too low to constitute a real form of compulsion. On the other hand, whoever participates in a jury receives a small monetary compensation.

In the case concerning the assassination of the Jesuits, it was feared that it might be impossible to put together a jury, due to the reigning political situation in the country, the parties involved in the case, and the menacing climate surrounding the affair. Throughout the entire proceedings, various security measures were taken to prevent the names of the jurors from becoming known publicly. Despite the dangers, and in an excellent demonstration of civic spirit, on the day fixed for the public hearing seven of the persons convoked (a larger number had been summoned) appeared in court, leading to the setting up of a jury composed of three women and two men, with a sixth person attending the proceedings as an alternate. The judge directed the procedure in the presence of lawyers representing the Private Accusation (the victims' families and the university), the prosecutor's office, and the defense.

The manner in which Salvadoran procedural law governs the means by which the jury must form a convinced opinion and translate that conviction into a verdict (art. 363 CPP) constituted, in the opinion of the ICJ observer, and as will be seen below, one of the central problems concerning the outcome of this trial.

On the morning of Thursday, September 26, 1991, in the premises of the Supreme Court of Justice in San Salvador, the jury was constituted and the public trial began. Amid an impressive array of security measures and a considerable deployment of police, the public entered the hearing room after an identity check at the door. At noon the judge opened the trial.

The members of the public attending the trial (only those with prior judicial authorization were allowed to enter the courtroom) amounted to approximately 100 persons divided into three groups: a) those associated with the party offended by the crime; b) various national and international observers; and c) family members of the accused. Earlier, members of the national and international press had been seated in a slightly elevated section of the hall. In the first row facing the public, and with their backs to the judge, sat the eight detained defendants, wearing their military uniforms and sporting their medals and decorations. To the right were the lawyers for the defense and for the party of the "Private Accusation." Behind the

accused and to the right sat the attorneys of the public prosecutor's office, and in the same row but to the center, the judge
and his collaborators. To the left, protected by a screen from
the sight of the public and the accused, was the jury. This mea-
sure of hiding the jurors from view was taken to protect them
from possible reprisals in case they were identified and to safe-
guard them from any kind of pressure.

There were 17 foreign observers from various universities
and international organizations, an exceptionally large number
of such persons for a criminal trial. In addition, numerous
members of the accredited diplomatic corps in El Salvador were
present, as were an important contingent of representatives
from the mass media (television, radio, and the press), demonstrating the keen interest with which the trial was being followed both inside the country and abroad.

On behalf of the ICJ as well as of himself, the observer wishes
to express publicly his gratitude and appreciation to the Salvadoran authorities for having provided him with every opportunity necessary to observe the trial, and for having done
so correctly and courteously. To the best of his knowledge,
the same opportunities were afforded to all of the observers
present.

The Bill of Indictment [arts. 329 and 349 CPP]

The bill of indictment, summarizing the elements to be treated
during the trial, is prepared by the judge and includes the evidence relating to the commission of the crime and the involvement of the accused, as well as any circumstances absolving or
modifying their criminal responsibility. Those passages which
the judge deems important for the adequate information of the
jury are read aloud in court.

The reading of the document by the judge's assistants took a
total of 15 hours and included more than 50 pieces of evidence,
with a recess being provided at midday and in the evening to
allow the jury and the various parties in the case to rest.
Throughout the three days that the public trial lasted, the daily
schedule was exhausting: from 8:30 in the morning to mid-
night.

It was a repetitive reading, since the declarations and confessions of each of the accused were read practically three times: i.e., their extrajudicial confession plus the judicial declarations of each of the two witnesses present at the confession. The witnesses were not asked whether what was contained in the rec- ord conformed to what the accused had confessed, but rather to repeat word for word what they had heard. The weakness of such a procedure is apparent: the witness of a statement concerning events in which he himself did not participate is not in a position to remember for days afterwards point by point what the person who made the statement said. Thus, the record becomes vulnerable to debate.

It is to be criticized, in our opinion, that among the passages read to the jurors there was no mention of the declarations made to the court by the accused in which they retracted their earlier extrajudicial confessions. We believe that an omission of this kind can confuse the jury. We also wish to point out that the bill of indictment provided no clear explanation of the circumstances which modified the criminal responsibility of the defendants nor the different levels of endangerment involved in each of these. There must be no doubt whatsoever in the mind of someone judging a defendant accused of committing a crime while carrying out orders, that the person acted to afflict his victim, exceeding the orders received and demonstrating a particular degree of endangerment (Private Oscar Amaya Grimaldi not only executed three priests in accordance with his "duty," but also fired at two others who had already been shot by Sub-Sergeant Avalos Vargas; he later appropriated the wristwatch of one of the dead men—a detail which he admitted in his own confession—and went to the kitchen near the scene of the crime to tranquilly drink a beer, subsequently joining the others in firing against the building, himself launching an anti-tank rocket).

In short, the record of indictment provided details concerning the judicial inspections at the scene of the crime, the medical examinations carried out on the bodies, the ballistics tests made of the weapons, spent cartridges, and remains of grenades discovered at the site; the appraisal requested by the civil party concerning the amount of damages caused to the premises (estimated at some $43,500); the extrajudicial confessions of the accused and the sworn depositions of the witnesses present at these confessions; the declarations of other witnesses living in nearby houses, and of the UCA watchmen, concerning what they had seen or heard; statements of other military personnel, some of whom had participated in the "operation" but who were not prosecuted, like Sergeant Eduardo Córdoba Montes ("the Savage") of the Atlacatl Battalion. This soldier acknowledged having participated in the search at the Jesuits' residence on the night of the 13th and later in the operations undertaken on the night of the 15th and 16th, and, although he did not admit responsibility for the crimes, he did describe the trip to the UCA as well as the place where he was posted with his patrol. There were also statements by Col. Benavides' superiors explaining the creation of the Security Command and what this implied, and a report from the CIHD concerning the steps taken in the investigation.

When the exhausting reading of the bill of indictment was finished, the judge asked the jurors whether they wished to personally question the accused or any of the witnesses. Art. 350 of the Code of Criminal Procedure authorizes jurors to "directly interrogate any of the defendants, offended parties, witnesses, or experts who have appeared in the bill of indictment." The jury, however, did not make use of this power and no questions were asked.

The Public Prosecutor suggested that the jurors travel to the scene of the crime to get a more complete picture of the events. The jurors replied through the judge that they did not wish to go, since they were already familiar with the place.

The Debates

As none of the various parties had requested declarations from additional witnesses, the stage was set for the beginning of the "debates" (art. 356 CPP). This involves what is known in other countries as the arguments of the prosecution and the defense. The prosecutor, acting in the name of society (which has been offended by the crime), summarizes the facts which he considers proven, as well as the specific responsibility of each of the accused in reference to the criminal laws violated, and ends by calling for application of the appropriate penalty involved. It is then the turn of the defense to contest the facts alleged, lay stress on others not taken into account by the prosecution or the judge, invoke specific exonerating or extenuating circumstances, request a verdict of acquittal or accept or dispute the penalty demanded by the prosecution, and even question the juridical qualification of the facts presented by the judge or the prosecutor.

This is also the moment for the "private accusation" to advance its argument, in systems which accept this institution for crimes pursuable ex-officio. Similarly, if the accusation has demanded indemnity for damages caused as the result of the crime, it must present its arguments now in support of such claims.

In the Salvadoran procedural system, an invitation to orally present their arguments is accorded to the parties in the following order: first the private accusation, when there is one, next the Public Prosecutor of the Republic, and finally the defense, with each of the parties being given the right of reply in a second round (art. 356 CCP). In accordance with the law, the judge allotted three hours to the private accusation, three hours to the prosecution, and six hours to the defense to present their respective arguments. For the right to reply, the time accorded was two hours for the private accusers, two hours for the prosecution, and four hours for the defense. While this, of course, considerably extended the length of the public hearing and therefore the "isolation" of the jury, it had the advantage in a case of such sensitivity and importance for public opinion of giving the various parties ample opportunity to explain their points of view in trying to convince the jury.

The "Private Accusation"

Attorneys Henry Campos and Sidney Blanco (ex-members of the prosecution in the same case, as we have seen) made their arguments to the jury, representing the families of the victims and the UCA. Their interventions were energetic and emotional, which seems to be customary practice in the Salvadoran judicial system, since the other parties acted in the same manner. They presented the facts in a didactic form, utilizing a map indicating the location of the UCA and the military security zone in which the university premises were situated. They indicated the route taken by the commandos, their regrouping points, and the specific role played, according to the attorneys, by each of the accused. They made logical reference to each piece of evidence gathered during the investigation, insisting on the importance of the defendants' extrajudicial confessions, the validity of which had been established not only by the Criminal Court, but also by the appeals court, the First Chamber of Criminal Law, and the Supreme Court of Justice.

Attorneys Campos and Blanco presented the events as having stemmed directly from a decision taken by the high command, with Col. Benavides as the officer charged with executing the decision. To this effect, they said, the colonel elaborated a careful plan, assigning individual tasks and roles to the military personnel under his orders. They affirmed that the colonel was responsible for having ordered the operation, but that he also was guilty by omission, citing art. 22 of the Criminal Code (Commission by omission: "He who neglects to prevent a result that in accordance with the circumstances he should and could have prevented, is as responsible as if he had produced the result himself"). They insisted that there had been other "intellectual authors" of the crimes, who remained in the shadows, but that as a beginning the nine accused soldiers should be punished; later perhaps the others could also be brought to justice.

The lawyers for the Private Accusation invoked the Geneva Convention of 1949 concerning Human Rights, in particular art. 30, as well as the Second Additional Protocol, which seeks to protect the victims of armed conflicts of a non-international character. It was the only concrete invocation of international law, although circumstantial reference was made to the assassinations as crimes against humanity.

With respect to the demand for indemnification of the parties affected by the action, the Private Accusation requested: a) for the UCA, payment to cover specific damages caused to the equipment, computers, premises, etc., a figure juridically assessed at some $45,400; b) for José Edgardo Ramos, son of Elba and brother of Celina, compensation estimated in the amount of $250,000; c) for the families of the Jesuits an entirely symbolic indemnification of one colón for each victim (which amounts to 12¢ per victim).

The action to secure monetary reparation was directed appropriately against the accused and against the Salvadoran state,[7] and was based legally on art. 245 of the Constitution, which establishes: "Functionaries and public employees will respond personally, and the State subsidiarily, for material or moral damages which they cause as a result of the violation of rights enshrined in this Constitution." Salvadoran law confirms the personal responsibility of the perpetrator of an act, and subsidiarily that of the State. Other systems on the continent (e.g., Uruguay) always insist on the direct responsibility of the State for the damages caused by its agents in the performance of their function, allowing the State to take action subsequently against the person responsible in order to recover the amount it was forced to pay out in damages.

Although the point was not cited by the lawyers for the Private Accusation, the ICJ observer wishes to point out that this primary responsibility of the State, with the consequent obligation to compensate and indemnify, is encoded in arts. 11 and 12 of the "Declaration on the Fundamental Principles of Justice for Victims of Crimes and Abuses of Power," adopted by the United Nations General Assembly on November 29, 1985 (Resolution 40/34). At the same time, the point is analyzed in a recent and valuable preliminary report prepared for the United Nations Sub-Commission on the Prevention of Discrimination and Protection of Minors by a member of the Sub-Commission, Professor Theodore van Boven ("Compensation for Victims of Serious Violations of Human Rights," U.N. document E/CN.4/Sub.2/1991/7). In the case concerning the assassination of the Jesuits, the crimes were committed by governmental agents (military personnel) during the exercise of their functions.

The lawyers for the Private Accusation ended their argument by requesting the jury—which they called the "tribunal of con-

---

[7] The insolvency of the accused was confirmed during the course of the trial, as was the fact that in January 1990, i.e., several days before his arrest, Col. Benavides sold the property in which he lived with his family.

science"—to respond affirmatively to each of the 80 questions, which the judge would formulate at the end of the debate, concerning the responsibility of the nine defendants vis-a-vis the charges for which they were being judged.

The Prosecutor General of the Republic

It was then the turn of the prosecutor's office, as the organ accusing the defendants in the name of Salvadoran society offended by the crime. The time assigned to the prosecution was divided among three of its attorneys, Mssrs. Eduardo Pineda Valenzuela, Saúl Zelaya Castillo, and Edwin Bonilla. Other lawyers from the public prosecutor's office stayed in the hall to collaborate with their colleagues.

The arguments of the prosecution were equally energetic, delivered in the vehement rhetorical style which, as we have already noted, is customary practice in the Salvadoran legal profession. The prosecutor, Mr. Pineda Valenzuela, qualified the attitude of the military men interrogated during the course of the investigation as constituting an "enormous conspiracy of silence." They were soldiers and officers, he said, who saw nothing, heard nothing, knew nothing; and who obstructed the investigation. He described the murdered Jesuits as men crying out for peace and justice, whose "only crime was that of thinking differently than the military."

Mr. Zelaya Castillos exhibited the arms used in the crime (the AK-47 rifle and the M-60 machine gun). He stressed that a huge battle had been simulated where in fact there had been no battle, utilizing weapons of Soviet manufacture characteristic of the guerrillas and not employed by the Armed Forces, but which the Military Academy had in its possession. These weapons had caused enormous destruction to the premises of the Center of Theology. After officials at the Academy denied the presence of such weapons in their school, the prosecutor's office had been able to establish that they indeed had at their disposal four AK-47s, one of which was the rifle that killed three of the Jesuits. The only objective of this aspect of the operation was to cast blame for the assassinations on the FMLN.

Mr. Edwin Bonilla maintained that the crime had been prepared in advance, and as the colonel had insisted that "he did not want any witnesses," the soldiers had killed everybody they found on the premises, including the two women. He then addressed the accused one by one, describing each man's participation in the events and detailing in a loud voice the precise circumstances of each assassination. The prosecuting attorney stressed the cruelty used, referring to the "ostentatious barbarity with which they acted."

Many local jurists concurred in pointing out to the ICJ observer that the attitude of the public prosecutor's office had evolved favorably following the decision in June 1990 by the Legislative Assembly to designate Dr. Roberto Mendoza Jérez as Prosecutor General in replacement of the disputed Mauricio Colorado. Earlier, during the instruction phase of the process, the public prosecutor's office had harshly attacked the Director of the Legal Protection Office of the Archdiocese of San Salvador, María Julia Hernández, for "impeding the advance of justice." According to the prosecutor's office, she had concealed evidence in the present case (several spent cartridges), a groundless accusation not taken into account by the judge. The Prosecutor had also joined the Defense in its efforts to have the case removed from Judge Zamora and given to the Court of Santa Tecla, arguing that territorial reasons dictated that the latter tribunal should be the one to try the case. These attempts also were in vain.

Returning to the public hearing: the representatives of the prosecutor's office ended their argument by declaring that the offenses in this case, which they characterized as crimes against humanity, must not go unpunished, and they called upon the jury, whom they termed the "court of the people," to respond with a YES to each of the 80 questions that the judge would formulate, given that the prosecution had amply demonstrated the proof of all the accusations.

The Defense

The Defense consisted of a group of lawyers headed by Dr. Carlos Méndez Flores, with whom collaborated Raúl Méndez Castro, José Adalfredo Salgado, and Eulogio Rodríguez Barahona. The latter collaborator is not a lawyer but a student of law, as the Salvadoran system (art. 63 CPP) authorizes that the role of defender in criminal cases be discharged not only by attorneys but also by law students who have passed specific courses. These four conducted the defense for all of the accused, a fact that seems a bit curious considering that specific points in some of their declarations were mutually contradictory (e.g., Lieutenants Espinoza and Mendoza accused each other of having commanded the group that carried out the actions).

The plan of the Defense in the public trial, as became evident, included a defense and eulogy of the Armed Forces, in particular the Atlacatl Rapid Reaction Battalion. In this connection, the Defense had arranged for the service records of the accused to be added to the trial documentation, pointing up their military merits, level of training, and combat experience. They also made recourse to a series of arguments praising nationalist values and resistance to what they termed "foreign intervention" (i.e., the pressure applied on El Salvador to conduct this trial and to produce a guilty verdict). At the same time they harshly attacked the FMLN, the Jesuits at the UCA, and the Society of Jesus as a whole. Nor were attacks lacking against foreign governments, in particular Spain and the United States, and against the observers who had come from abroad to attend the trial.

The observer was surprised at how little of the time accorded to the Defense (six hours for the argument and four hours for the reply) was used to question the evidence advanced as proof of the charges against the defendants. The discourse of the defense attorneys was primarily centered on asserting and repeating that the accused "were never at the UCA" and therefore did not take part in the operation of assassination and attack against the Center of Theology. This explains why the Defense never invoked "hierarchic obedience to orders issued by superiors" as grounds for the lack of guilt of the defendants (art. 40, c, CP). This reasoning was never invoked simply because, according to the defense attorneys, the defendants never participated in the acts of which they were accused. We will see later, however, how this aspect of the question may have had a decisive influence on the verdict.

Turning to the incriminating evidence, the Defense limited itself to arguing that the extrajudicial confessions were not valid because: a) they were given more than 72 hours after the arrest of the accused (art. 496, 1 CPP); b) the defendants denied their validity before the judge, maintaining that they had been intimidated and forced into accepting the confessions by the agents of the CIHD (though the defense attorneys did not question why the two eyewitnesses present at the confessions declared to the judge that the statements had been given freely); c) persons who are co-authors or accomplices in the same crime or offence may not appear as witnesses against one other (art. 499 CPP); d) Col. Benavides had been accused solely in his capacity as Head of the Security Command. The defense attorneys also objected to the interpretation given by the prosecutor's office and the Court to the technical expertise provided, such as autopsies, ballistics tests, and graphological analysis of the placard left in the residence of the Jesuits implicating the FMLN.

The first member of the defense team to speak was attorney Rodríguez Barahona, who did so in high-sounding terms. Among the curious characteristics of his legal argumentation was that of occasionally addressing "Salvadorans who are listening to us on radio or TV." Carrying out the plan of the defense, Mr. Barahona paid fiery tribute to the Armed Forces, stressing how much the Salvadoran nation "needs valiant people like these," and delivered several mystical-religious invocations whose pertinence to the current trial completely escaped the ICJ observer. He embarked on an attack against three persons attending the debate: the Provincial for Central America of the Society of Jesus, Father José María Tojeira; the Rector of the UCA, Father Miguel F. Estrada; and the Director of the Legal Protection Office of the Archdiocese of San Salvador, María Julia Hernández. Mr. Barahona accused them all of having interfered with the police investigations. He ended by referring to the 500 years of the "Spanish presence" on the continent, and to the fact that he himself had native blood (*sangre "pipil"*) and therefore had the courage to defend the accused; that a verdict of innocent would serve "to demonstrate to the Jesuits, the Spanish, and the Churches that here there is justice." To the surprise of the ICJ observer, the judge remained impassive in the face of these remarks, tolerating insults against third persons and institutions and not even reminding the defense attorney that his argumentation had strayed too far from the object of the trial.

He was followed by Dr. Méndez Castro, who also referred to the "noble institution" of the Armed Forces, pointing out that without the military even the judge would not be able to exercise his authority, and calling attention to the decorations and metals worn by the accused. Dr. Castro mentioned the intolerable "international pressure" being exercised upon the Salvadoran justice system, reminding his listeners that the United States Congress had interrupted part of its military assistance to the country, conditioning its restoration on the convening of the present trial.

Dr. Castro described the processing of the case as filled with irregularities. His argument centered particularly on the charges of crimes of terrorism. Addressing himself to the jury, which he termed the "tribunal of conscience," he told them that they should not ratify what the lawyers for the private accusation and the prosecution had said, but rather that they should reach a verdict only in accordance with their own conscience. The Armed Forces could not commit the crime of terrorism, since their task was itself to combat terrorism. Moreover, the Armed Forces was not a clandestine institution (referring to art. 402 CP). Dr. Castro completed his argument by affirming that "we Salvadorans can solve our own problems without foreign interference" and urging the jury to answer NO to each of the 80 questions that the judge would formulate.

The third attorney for the defense was José A. Salgado, who tried to discredit the juridically validated extrajudicial confessions as having no relevance to the charge of "acts in preparation of terrorism" (art. 402 CP). He attempted to show that the alleged meeting of the officers with Col. Benavides on the night of the 15th was a fabrication. Mr. Salgado's oration was perhaps the most aggressive against the Jesuits as an institution. He asserted that the Jesuits "rule the world," that they "control congresses," and that "they are interested in destabilizing the Government." The fact that delegations of Jesuits and foreign observers were present did not mean that a verdict of guilty must be reached. In some respects, Salgado's discourse came close to being a kind of justification for the murders, though of course without saying this. Again the judge remained impassive, until the Public Prosecutor formally protested the insults that were being cast. Only then did the magistrate indicate to the defense attorney that what he was saying was "a matter outside the framework of the trial."

At the end of this speech, the judge pointed out that Mr. Salgado had been appointed to represent the absent defendant (Pvt. Sierra Ascencio) in an official capacity, and that therefore he must speak in defense of the soldier, having not yet referred to the case. This gave rise to several references by Salgado concerning the defendant.

The last of the attorneys to present the argument of the defense was the leader of the team, Dr. Carlos Méndez Flores. He began by saying that Salvadorans (and therefore the jury) must not "capitulate in the face of foreign pressure," and he referred concretely to the Congress of the United States and to Spain (it should be remembered that the Spanish ambassador and a delegation from the Spanish parliament were present in the hall). He then recalled the conditions experienced during the FMLN offensive in November 1989, when in the capital alone some 2,000 persons died, adding that at that moment "the international observers should have come to see if they could stop the offensive." Dr. Méndez Flores further pointed out that the military men who were being judged in the case had risked their lives in defense of everyone, including the foreign observers. Addressing himself to the members of the public present, he stated, "You internationalists do not understand what we are going through in El Salvador." But of course "the Salvadoran dead do not interest you,"—a thinly veiled reference to the Spanish nationality of several of the murdered priests.

Dr. Méndez Flores continued by criticizing various analyses of the events at the UCA made by the Jesuit Provincial, Father Tojeira, and the UCA Deacon, Father Estrada, which had been published in the press, and he again accused them, as well as María Julia Hernández, of attempting to undertake investigations on their own, substituting themselves for the legitimate organs of the state.

Dr. Méndez Flores ended by harshly calling into question the procedures followed by the Comisión de Investigación de Hechos Delictivos (CIHD), stating that they had invented and fabricated various facts and details and had faked the evidence. Addressing the prosecutor, he said, "You always lie." He called on the jury to respond with 80 categorical NO's to the questions that the judge was going to pose.

While his argumentation was proceeding, there was a public demonstration in front of the Supreme Court building involving a group of some 200 persons with banners and placards that read, for example, "The Armed Forces have the support of the people" and "When the communist offensive comes, who is going to defend the people?" Using bullhorns, the crowd loudly demanded a verdict of acquittal. Participating in the demonstration were family members of the accused and wounded military personnel. Their voices could be heard inside the courtroom.

The Rebuttals

Initiating this second round of interventions, the lawyers for the Private Accusation contested a number of assertions made by the defense attorneys. They insisted that the accusations against the defendants were based for the most part on their own confessions, which had been validated by all levels of judicial authority, including the Supreme Court. They then read out parts of the report prepared by Scotland Yard, in which that police body concluded that the perpetrators of the action had sought to distance themselves from the deeds and minimize their participation by concealing information. One of the attorneys for the Private Accusation (H. Campos) said that following the reasoning of the Defense, it could be concluded that until peace was reached in El Salvador, the military had a licence to kill in any circumstance. They concluded their rebuttal by again asking the jury to issue a verdict of guilty for all of the accused; this would make it possible later to identify other persons responsible at higher levels.

The sole spokesman for the prosecution was Dr. Saúl Zelaya, who noted that it was not the Armed Forces as an institution that was being judged, but only those of its members who had committed a horrible crime. He protested against the defamatory accusations launched against the Jesuits present in the hall and indicated that attempts had been made to ridicule them. He added that it had emerged from the trial that Lt. Mendoza had left the residence of the Jesuits with a satchel (which he had not brought with him to the site), and that this could have contained the missing $5,000 of the Alfonso Comín prize, which Father Ellacuría had received in Barcelona. Finally Dr. Zelaya pointed to the assertion by the Armed Forces that the soldier ("Chiquiton") who fired the M-60 machine gun at the Center of Theology and the one who had moved the dead body at the order of Lt. Espinoza had both died in combat at the village of Mejicanos, and that Captain Herrera Carranza, who could have provided some clarifying elements, had been killed in San Francisco Gotera. He wondered whether these deaths had really occurred in the manner claimed or whether there had been an attempt to eliminate witnesses. Dr. Zelaya ended by requesting a verdict of guilty for all of the accused and on each of the charges for which they had been indicted.

Three of the defense attorneys spoke in rebuttal. They again voiced xenophobic arguments and appealed to nationalist sentiment: if the jury found the accused not guilty, "we will show the world that in El Salvador justice is done." Dr. Méndez Flores said that the colonel could not be held responsible for what his subordinates might have done; if any of them had committed a crime, then it was that person himself who must face the penal consequences of his misconduct: responsibility is always personal. He again harshly criticized international interference in the case, and said that the most powerful nation meddling in the affair was the one who had committed the most violations against human rights, reminding the audience of the 5,000 victims caused by the invasion of Panama by the United States to capture General Noriega. Dr. Méndez Flores referred to the Armed Forces as the "glorious Salvadoran army," and concluded that it was only international pressure that was keeping the accused under arrest. He called on the jury to pronounce a verdict of not guilty for all of the accused, in this "trial of dignity."

At the close of the debates, the specific accusations against each of the defendants about which the jury had to pronounce a verdict were as follows:

- Colonel Guillermo Alfredo Benavides Moreno (Director of the Military Academy). Responsible as the mediate author (art. 46 CP) of the murder of the six Jesuit priests and the two women (art. 154 CP).[8] Responsible as the mediate author of acts in preparation of terrorism and acts of terrorism.
- Lieutenant Yusshy René Mendoza Vallecillos (Military Academy). Responsible as the immediate author (art 45 CP) of the murder of the eight victims (the six Jesuit priests and the two women). Responsible as the immediate author of acts in preparation of terrorism and acts of terrorism.
- Lieutenant José Ricardo Espinoza Guerra (of the Atlacatl Battalion). Responsible as the immediate author of the murder of the eight victims. Responsible for acts in preparation of terrorism and acts of terrorism.
- Second Lieutenant Gonzalo Guevara Cerritos (Atlacatl Battalion). Responsible as the immediate author of the murder of the eight victims. Responsible for acts in preparation of terrorism and acts of terrorism.
- Sub-Sergeant Ramiro Avalos Vargas (Atlacatl Battalion). Responsible as the immediate author of the murder of the eight victims. Responsible for acts in preparation of terrorism and acts of terrorism.
- Sub-Sergeant Tomás Zarpate Castillos (Atlacatl Battalion). Responsible for the same crimes and in the same capacity as Sub-Sargeant Avalos Vargas.
- Corporal Angel Pérez Vázquez (Atlacatl Battalion). Responsible for the same crimes and in the same capacity as Avalos and Zarpate.

---

[8] Murder is a particularly serious form of homicide, which applies, as in the present case, when it can be proven that the authors have acted with treachery and premeditation. Immediate authors are those who directly commit the crime; mediate authors are those who compel, cause, or order others to commit the crime.

- Private Oscar Mariano Amaya Grimaldi (Atlacatl Battalion). Responsible for the same crimes and in the same capacity as Avalos, Zarpate, and Pérez.
- Private Jorge Alberto Sierra Ascencio (fugitive; Atlacatl Battalion). Responsible for the murders of Elba Ramos and her daughter Celina.

The four officers (Benavides, Mendoza, Espinoza, and Guevara) were also prosecuted for the crime of inciting and conspiring to commit acts of terrorism (art. 403 CP). The rest of the defendants, as rank and file soldiers and non-commissioned officers, were not charged with this offense, since they did not participate in the meeting with Col. Benavides on November 15th. In accordance with procedural law, this crime will be judged directly by the magistrate, without the need for participation by the jury.

At 5 P.M. on Saturday, September 28th, the judge declared the adjournment of the public hearing. He then ordered the participating parties and the public to leave the hall and the guards to remove the prisoners. This having been done, the jury went into deliberation.

THE VERDICT

The Code of Criminal Procedure (CPP) contains a rule (art. 363) in the chapter governing the activity of the jurors which, partly through the text itself and partly through the interpretation given it in Salvadoran jurisprudence, permitted the issuing of a completely arbitrary verdict and one which, in the view of the ICJ observer as well as that of other international observers, cannot be qualified as just.

The law does not ask jurors to explain how they arrived at their conviction; the law does not prescribe the rules by which they must infer the adequacy of a piece of evidence; it does require them to question themselves in silence and concentration and to seek in the sincerity of their conscience what impression has been made upon their minds by the evidence produced both against the accused and in their defense. The law does not say, "take this fact as true"; it poses one question covering the extent of the jurors' responsibilities: "Do you have a personal conviction? [art. 363 CPP]

The decision of the jury is formed by a majority of the votes of its five members; it is not clear from the verdict how many votes were in favor of the decision nor the names of the persons who cast these votes. The verdict "is not subject to appeal; but the parties may dispute any legal invalidities (nullities) that the verdict contains . . ." (art. 389 CPP). In general the grounds for legal invalidity are tied to faults of a formal nature, but one of these refers to cases in which "sufficient proof does not exist of the defendant's participation" (arts. 390 and 275 CPP).

After several hours of deliberation by the jury, the judge convoked the various parties, the observers, the press, the families of the accused, and the authorized public, who were waiting on the ground floor of the building, to return to the courtroom, where the verdict of the jury would be read.

The judge proceeded to read aloud the responses of either Yes or No to each of the 80 questions he had formulated to the jury: this involved one question concerning each of the accused for each of the crimes with which they were charged. The question was posed as follows: "Does the jury have the personal conviction that the defendant X is guilty as charged?"

Regarding the charge of murder, the jury found only two of the defendants guilty and acquitted the other seven men indicted. Concerning the crimes of terrorism, it found none of the nine soldiers guilty. In short, Colonel Guillermo Alfredo Benavides Moreno was found guilty of the eight murders (i.e., of the six Jesuits and the two women); the jury found Lieutenant Yusshy René Mendoza Vallecillos guilty of only one murder, that of the minor, Celina Mariset Ramos, acquitting him of the other seven murders. The other defendants were declared not guilty of any of the eight murders, and all nine of the soldiers were acquitted on the charges of terrorism.

For the observers the verdict was, to say the least, surprising, as both they and the jury had heard the confessions of the accused, in which they related clearly and in ample detail how they had executed their victims without the latter having put up the slightest resistance, and how they had partially destroyed the Center of Theology.

Chapter IV
CONCLUSIONS OF THE OBSERVER

The first observation would be to recall that the events that occasioned the indictments occurred in the middle of an offensive launched by the FMLN against various cities throughout the country, and in particular the capital, San Salvador. This must have played an important role in the decision to assassinate the six Jesuits.

For its part, the judicial process took place in a context of civil war marked by intense armed combat, despite the progress achieved in the peace negotiations held between the Government and the FMLN. This situation made it difficult to arrive at a just outcome, and in fact we believe that such an outcome did not result. In the end the context of war conditioned the trial.

It is also important to emphasize a very positive aspect: the crimes for which the military men were indicted were considered at all times as *offenses against common law* and thus subject to civil jurisdiction. Even if this was only proper and fitting, we emphasize it here because in many countries during situations of acute internal conflict, cases such as this one tend to be brought before military courts, with the result that a satisfactory outcome is not attained from the point of view of justice. A solution which is gaining ground in various international fora—and which enjoys the support of the ICJ—is that when it is a matter involving a transgression against common law, military personnel should be subject to the same justice as the rest of the population. Military justice should be applied only in cases of crimes which violate specifically military obligations, i.e., actions which are not offenses when committed by a civilian (e.g., insubordination or desertion).

The observer believes that during the course of the judicial procedure, the manner in which the events occurred was amply and clearly proven beyond a doubt, as was described fully by the Lawyers Committee for Human Rights in New York, the Central American Provincial of the Society of Jesus, and the Instituto de Derechos Humanos de la Universidad Centro-americana de San Salvador (the Human Rights Institute of the Central American University in San Salvador—IDHUCA). We have extracted material from various publications of these bodies, incorporating it in Chapter II: The Events.

With respect to the investigation of the facts (the *sumario*), the observer is forced to conclude that the authority entrusted with the task of investigating the case, the Comisión de Investigación de Hechos Delictivos (Commission for the Investigation of Criminal Acts), did not carry out its work in an adequate manner, neglecting to undertake a series of procedures customary in criminal cases, thereby allowing evidence to be lost and even intentionally destroyed and affording the suspects the time to formulate their alibis. In general the CIHD showed a lack of interest in arriving at the truth. This attitude changed after the report issued by the Comisión de Honor de la Fuerza Armada, to whom the law does not assign powers of investigation in legal cases but whose report undoubtedly permitted nine culprits to materialize, although at the same time limiting the investigation to these nine. From that moment on, the CIHD investigated in depth, but only with respect to the nine persons eventually indicted. It seems to have not wished to look in other spheres.

From our point of view, it is unfortunate that the detectives who make up the CIHD are subject to military regulations and that their chiefs are military officers. The police should be a civil body, totally independent of the Armed Forces.

In any case, we consider that both in the investigative stage as well as in the trial the following facts were fully proven:

- That the crime was agreed upon, decided, and planned during a meeting held in Col. Benavides' office at the Military Academy on the night of November 15, 1989. That on this occasion the colonel gave precise orders concerning the execution of the crime to his subordinates Lieutenants Mendoza and Espinoza and Sub-Sgt. Guevara Cerritos (putting Mendoza in charge of the operation because of his grade). That these orders consisted of eliminating the Jesuits (particularly Father Ignacio Ellacuría) because, as the colonel told his men, the Jesuits of the UCA were the ringleaders of the guerrilla insurgency, were the intellectuals that directed it, were terrorists, and that the soldiers must also eliminate anyone else whom they encountered at the site ("I don't want any witnesses"). The criminal responsibility of the colonel does not derive—as the First Chamber of Criminal Law (Camera Primera de lo Penal) erroneously stated in its ruling of April 9, 1991—from his capacity as Chief of the Security Command, but rather for having given such orders as Chief.

- That the order to kill was not given at the spur of the moment in the middle of combat, but coldly, with reflection and premeditation, and that those who received the order had several hours to consider it carefully, to appreciate its obviously illegal character, and to foresee the consequences of their acts.

- That the officers in charge went with their men to the UCA, mounting a vast and complex operation in which some 80 soldiers participated, providing cover and support for the action of the commandos. That the operation was carried out in the most fully patrolled and controlled zone of the city, where it would have been practically impossible for a troop movement to escape notice. That prior to their arrival and also at the spot, the officers explained to their subordinates the action and role each one of them was to carry out (both those subsequently indicted and others who were not brought to trial), so that all the participants knew exactly what they were doing.

- That the group selected for the operation consisted of commandos from the Atlacatl Rapid Reaction Battalion, all of them specially trained in counterinsurgency warfare in the United States, and who had been sent to the capital on November 12th due to the military offensive launched by the FMLN. That this force had been placed under the exclusive responsibility of Col. Benavides. That the same day the colonel had been appointed by the military high command as Chief in Command of the Security Zone, an area which included militarily strategic positions in the city of San Salvador, and in which the UCA was also located.

- That the operation was prepared in advance by means of a search of the premises—a reconnaissance mission, as it were—undertaken the night of November 13th by the very men who later carried out the assassinations.
- That everything was planned to make the operation seem like an action of the FMLN, which included using arms (e.g., an AK-47 rifle of Soviet manufacture) utilized by the guerrillas but not by the Armed Forces, mounting an attack with heavy weaponry against the Center of Theology to simulate a battle, and at the end of the operation leaving a notice written by one of the commandos, in which the FMLN claimed responsibility for the "execution."
- That both the AK-47 rifle as well as the M-60 machine gun used in the attack came from the Military Academy, and that the decision to take them out of the Academy could only have been authorized by the director, Col. Benavides. That there were other examples of complicity following the crime—to cite only one example: the destruction of the registers in which were recorded troop movements to and from the Military Academy and which could have confirmed the departure and return of the Atlacatl commandos on the night of the events (as a result, a lieutenant colonel is now facing trial on charges of "actual concealment" for having destroyed evidence).
- That regarding the concrete execution of the assassinations, the accused confessed clearly and in abundant detail to their participation, without the defense having been able to prove its allegations that the confessions were extracted by violence or intimidation. The main points in this regard include:

  a) that Sub-Sergeant Ramiro Avalos Vargas assassinated Fathers Juan Ramón Moreno and Amando López;
  b) that Private Oscar Amaya Grimaldi assassinated Fathers Ignacio Ellacuría, Ignacio Martín-Baró, and Segundo Montes;

c) that Sub-Sergeant Tomás Zarpate Castillos fired at the mother and daughter, Elba and Celina Mariset Ramos, leaving them for dead; that finally both women were shot dead by Private Jorge Sierra Ascencio;

d) that Corporal Angel Pérez Vásquez killed Father Joaquín López y López;

e) that Lieutenants Yusshy Mendoza and José Ricardo Espinoza directed the operation, assisted by Second Lieutenant Gonzalo Guevara Cerritos, and that all three of the officers received their orders from Colonel Guillermo Benavides Moreno.

- That the manner in which the killings were carried out reveals a great disregard for life as well as the dangerousness of the authors of the crime, the latter having cold-bloodedly murdered persons who offered no resistance and who were completely defenseless (lying face down on the grass), and having not hesitated to kill a woman and a 15-year-old girl for the simple accidental reason that they found them there.
- That regarding the terrorist attack against the Center of Theology, committed with the sole objective of implicating the FMLN, all but one of the accused admitted having participated in the attack, with varying degrees of responsibility. Colonel Benavides was the only one who did not admit his participation, despite the fact that it was proved that he planned the operation and ordered it to be carried out.

The proof of the charges, which undoubtedly should have led any court of law to convict the accused, emerges primarily from their own confessions. Although these confessions were made to the police (CIHD), and thus are considered extrajudicial, they remain valid in the eyes of the law by virtue of art. 496 of the Code of Criminal Procedure, since two eyewitnesses to the confessions testified before the magistrate to having been present when the statements were given. In addition the confessions were truthful, consistent, detailed, and in "concordance with other existing elements of the case in a trial concerning the same punishable offense" (art. 496), i.e., in accord with the other declarations and confessions, the ballistics tests, the types of weapons used, the results of the autopsies, etc. Their validity was not undermined simply because later in declarations made before the judge the accused retracted their confessions and denied having been at the UCA. These subsequent statements did not furnish the slightest convincing element that might call into question the validity of the confessions, and the assertions by their attorneys that they had been intimidated and forced by agents of the CIDH to make the original declarations did not succeed in demolishing the wealth of detail with which they had explained the role performed by each one of them in the operation. Moreover, this point was settled in the *plenario* by Criminal Judge No. 4, by the First Chamber of Criminal Law, and by the Supreme Court, all of which led to the confessions being accepted as valid.

As regards the legal stipulation not allowing the statements of one witness to be used against another when both persons "are coauthors or accomplices in the same offense" (art. 499 CPP), the magistrates maintained both in the first as well as the second appeal that these elements of the confessions had not been taken into account. In another part of the present report, the observer has already criticized this rule that prevents such testimony to be considered, deeming it to be not conducive to the goal of establishing the truth.

The observer likewise has criticized another legal provision, that of art. 205 of the Code of Criminal Procedure, which allows certain dignitaries of the state, including "officers of the armed forces with the rank of general or colonel," not to appear in person to testify before the court but rather to make their declarations in writing. In the present trial, the fact that various high-ranking military officers took advantage of this exemption from the general rule on appearing clearly limited the possibilities of investigation.

As regards the different types of crimes with which the accused were charged, in the opinion of the observer, the charge of murder (art. 154 CP) was correct, since especially serious cases of homicide were involved. This crime used to be punished with the death penalty, but fortunately the Constitution of 1983 in its article 27 abolished this form of punishment in cases of common law (it can be applied only for military offenses "during a state of international war"), at the same time that it abolished "life sentences." The law currently fixes the penalty for murder at 20 to 30 years in prison. As we have said, all of the accused committed this offense with varying levels of responsibility; there was a "division of labor" involved, but a common criminal intent and unity in the conception and execution of the crime.

With respect to the crime of acts of terrorism (art. 400 CP), it is our opinion that all of the accused were guilty of this offense. They indeed committed "acts that can produce alarm, fear, or terror, utilizing: explosive or inflammable substances: arms or artifacts that normally are capable of causing damage to human life or limb. . . ." Moreover—the article continues—acts of terrorism include: "2.) Destruction or damage to public property, or property intended for public use" (the Center of Theology is intended for public use, even if the UCA is a private institution).

Where the observer disagrees with the magistrate is that if the authorship of the crime of "acts of terrorism" has been proven in the case of an individual, that person cannot be held responsible also for "acts in preparation of terrorism" (art. 402 CP), and even less for "inciting and conspiring to commit acts of terrorism" (art. 403 CP). This is because the three offenses form part of the same "*iter criminis*": once the most important of the three has been committed, previous acts are subsumed in it. By the same argument, the attempt at carrying out a crime cannot be punished in addition to the crime once it is actually committed. Punishment of "preparatory acts" or "inciting and conspiring" would be admissible only if the criminal terrorist action had not progressed beyond one of those two stages.

It was evident that the indictments for terrorism provoked considerable tension within the Armed Forces, which considered that its men could not commit this offense, applicable only to the armed opposition—a position without any juridical foundation.

As regards the proceedings of the public trial, the reading of the "*minuta*" (the record of indictment) was repetitive and confusing. It is not clear why those parts of the record in which the accused retracted their extrajudicial confessions were excluded from the reading. Nor was any indication given of their motives for doing so, which would have helped the jury judge the validity of their statements. In short, in the opinion of the observer, this was a procedure excessively attached to formalities and does not constitute a good method of informing the jury. The jury, for its part, did not ask to interrogate any of the accused, nor did the participating parties. This seems to be the general rule in public trials held in El Salvador.

During the course of the debates, the judge did not perform the role of orienting the discussions, but instead adopted an excessively passive attitude. In their argumentation and rebuttals, the different parties supported their assertions indiscriminately with admissible and inadmissible evidence alike, without the judge making any comment in this regard. This has the effect of creating a situation in which a popular jury, ignorant of judicial matters, has no way of distinguishing which pieces of evidence are valid for Salvadoran law and which are not. Thus, an important distinction is erased, one which had been carefully delineated by the Code of Criminal Procedure. We do not believe that this is the intended meaning of trial by jury.

The strategy of the defense lawyers consisted, as we have seen, of a spirited defense of the Salvadoran Armed Forces (though it was not the Armed Forces who were being judged in the trial), and of a markedly xenophobic appeal to an extreme nationalism and in favor of opposition to what the defense attorneys termed "foreign interference"—aspects that in no way formed the object of the trial. In any case, their line of argument, while not adequate in our view, was admissible. What is not admissible is that the judge tolerated serious attacks and slanderous statements on the part of the lawyers for the defense, which at some points took a threatening tone against persons unrelated to the actions being judged; against institutions (such as the Society of Jesus and the Jesuits as a whole, not only in El Salvador but throughout the world); against the governments of Spain and the United States; and against the observers who had come from outside the country to attend the trial. Despite this conduct, the judge presiding over the debates did not warn the defense lawyers, nor call on them to focus their statements exclusively on aspects related to the trial.

In general, beyond the problems mentioned it can be affirmed that all of the parties (the Private Accusation, the Prosecution, and the Defense) had every opportunity to present their arguments and carry out their respective tasks.

Regarding the verdict reached by the jury: herein lies the main failure of the judicial process. On the basis of article 363 CPP (quoted above) and the extensive interpretation given this article by Salvadoran jurisprudence, the verdict reached by the jury can only be characterized as arbitrary. In the opinion of this observer the text of article 363 is unclear and the conclusions drawn from the jurisprudence actually nullify its probable meaning. Even if the law does not require the jurors to "explain how they arrived at their conviction" and does not "prescribe the rules by which they must infer the adequacy of a piece of evidence," neither do these two points mean that they can simply disregard the Code of Criminal Procedure, and even less so the Criminal Code itself, ignoring the dispositions that govern criminal responsibility, the circumstances that can modify it, and the validity of the evidence that the law admits. To maintain the contrary, as seems to have been done in this trial, is to go against the sense of the law.

What is certain is that this manner of proceeding allows absurd results to occur, as in this case, in which seven of the accused were acquitted, despite having admitted fully, clearly, and in detail that they committed the offenses for which they were indicted and which revealed a singular threat to and disdain for human life. Even more absurd is the fact that Lieutenant Yusshy René Mendoza Vallecillos was found guilty of the murder of Celina Mariset Ramos but innocent of having killed her mother, when in fact both women died with their arms around each other, victims of the same bullets fired by the same hands, which furthermore were not those of the lieutenant.

What, then, could have been the elements on which the jury might have based its verdict? We do not know that, given the manner of proceeding which we have already commented upon, and consequently we can offer only hypothetical answers. One of the hypotheses is that a reasoning may have been applied which is more appropriate to the military than to civilians: punish those who gave illegitimate orders and exonerate those who carried them out.

If what the jury wanted was to apply the rule of "hierarchic obedience," under which orders are given by superiors in a context of rigid military discipline to which the subordinates are subject (elite troops fighting in a situation of civil war), then this would have to have been based on evidence that the soldiers were forced to execute the orders without discussing them. This would have formed "grounds for lack of guilt" according to Salvadoran criminal law (art. 40 CP), excluding criminal responsibility on the part of authors of the illicit act. As we said before, the defense attorneys did not invoke these grounds for exoneration, maintaining instead that their clients did not participate in the events and were not at the UCA, and that the colonel did not give orders at the supposed meeting on the night of the 15th, since this meeting itself never occurred.

But there is a central argument which would rule out the "hierarchic obedience" rationale. If the jury applied this stipulation—and we do not know whether it did—then it was applied badly. The same article 40 of the Criminal Code establishes in clause c) that for the "hierarchic obedience" argument to function, it is required, among other things, "that the order obviously not have the character of a punishable offense." And it cannot occur to anybody that the order to murder defenseless persons and to kill any witnesses that may be present, and to stage a mock battle in order to cast blame for the crime on the FMLN, a mock battle involving the destruction of property and public endangerment, could be legal and not punishable. That the operation was a punishable offense was obvious, no matter what the cultural level of those who received the orders or the degree of their understanding of the penal liabilities involved. Nor would application of the "hierarchic obedience" rule explain why Lt. Mendoza was found guilty of the murder of Celina M. Ramos, a minor, but not of her mother, or why the other seven defendants went free.

Another disturbing element concerning this way of "doing justice"—an element which may be incidental, but which in any case awakens suspicion since the jury's line of reasoning is not known—is the fact that the only two persons found guilty belonged to the Military Academy, while the other seven defendants acquitted belonged to the Atlacatl Battalion. It is as if the jury did not want to damage the "combat morale" of a battle-hardened unit like the Atlacatl only because some of its members had done something for which they unfortunately had been trained. But this is perhaps the only way to explain why, of the two lieutenants indicted, one was found guilty and the other innocent. It goes without saying that this kind of reasoning has no juridical basis proper to a correct administration of justice.

In short, the decision of the jurors resembled more the reasoning of the military than that of a civil jury.

SUMMARY ASSESSMENT

1. It is true that there was considerable international concern that the deaths of the Jesuit priests be investigated thoroughly and their authors brought to trial. And it was this international interest, demonstrated in many forms—including by United Nations bodies such as Subcommission on the Prevention of Discrimination and Protection of Minors[11], numerous non-governmental organizations (NGOs), and various parliaments, notably those of the United States and Spain—that made it possible for the events to be investigated and the trial finally held. But in the opinion of the ICJ observer, in this day and age in international fora concerned with the application of human rights, to demand justice as a means of preventing further violations is not to practice "improper interference in the internal affairs of the state." It is rather to make international law function. Moreover, various international treaties, such as the Amer-

---

[11] In its Resolution 1991/11 of 26/August/1991, after paying tribute to the process of peace negotiations undertaken by the government and the Farabundo Martí Front for National Liberation and the agreements already achieved through this process, the Subcommission exhorts the authorities to achieve "substantial progress in the judicial investigation and punishment of those guilty of the murders committed on September 16, 1989 in the Central American University." The Subcommission is a body of 26 human rights experts of various nationalities, chosen by member states, who act in a personal capacity and independent of their governments.

ican Convention on Human Rights and the International Pact on Civil and Political Rights, demand and oblige the Republic of El Salvador to investigate and judge violations of human rights and indemnify the victims, or their families if they have died. The State of El Salvador cannot escape these obligations as long as it takes part in these treaties (art. 144 of the National Constitution).

2. When the final outcome of a trial is neither just nor in conformity with the law, *it must be concluded that the trial itself was not just.* In the case under study, the result was essentially arbitrary.

3. Following the activity of the Commission of Honor of the Armed Forces, although nine suspects did appear, *the investigation remained circumscribed,* extending no farther than to the superior officer who gave the order to commandos, who executed it.

4. Despite its faults, the trial constituted a *breach in the massive wall of impunity* that up until now has protected members of the Salvadoran military for their violations of human rights, violations which include the killing of unarmed combatants and the massacre of defenseless civilians. The situation is different from that of the FMLN combatants, who are brought to trial when they are captured. The present case was the first time in the recent history of El Salvador that military men were judged and convicted—with the limitations already discussed—for violation of human rights. The trial was transmitted in its entirety by national television and radio and was covered on a daily basis by the written press. This was of considerable didactic value, as it permitted the entire population of the country to learn in detail what had happened at the UCA in November 1989. Even though questions were not put to the accused during the public hearing, the people were able to hear the reading of the confessions that they had made to the CIHD, and assess the actions of these members of the Armed Forces. To sum up, the trial constituted a partial crack in the wall of impunity but not a triumph of justice, as the evidence produced during the process required that the nine defendants be found guilty.

5. The observer believes that if an adequate functioning of the administration of justice is desired, it will be necessary to

introduce *modifications to judicial procedure* in order to make it more flexible and less devoted to formalities. But it will also be necessary above all to modify the rules governing the functioning of the jury, as well as of forensic practice, and to accord the judge the role of orienting the jurors without conditioning them, i.e., informing them of the basic procedural rules governing criminal responsibility, the circumstances that can modify it, and the rules of evidence that the law admits. As the process currently functions, an arbitrary verdict can too easily be reached in any kind of trial, not just in particularly sensitive cases.

The trial did not come to an end with the verdict of the jury. The judge must still pronounce his sentence on the basis of what the jury decided. That is to say, he must fix a penalty for Col. Benavides Moreno and Lt. Mendoza Vallecillos, who were found guilty, the first on eight counts of murder, the second on one. Punishment for the crime of murder is fixed at a minimum of 20 years and a maximum of 30 years in prison, the latter being the current maximum penalty in El Salvador for common-law offenses. Judge Zamora must also issue a ruling concerning the crimes of "inciting and conspiring to commit acts of terrorism" with which the four officers (Benavides, Mendoza, Espinoza, and Guevara) are charged, since, according to Salvadoran law, this offense is judged by the magistrate without requiring a jury. Several days after the end of the public trial Judge Zamora released four of the defendants (Avalos Vargas, Zarpate Castillos, Pérez Vázquez, and Amaya Grimaldi; Sierra Ascencio was still a fugitive) in fulfillment of the verdict pronounced by the jury.

In accordance with the law, the judge has 30 days from the end of the public trial to pronounce a sentence and to issue a ruling on the amount of civil reparation demanded by the family members of the victims and by UCA; this latter ruling must include a decision about specifically who will receive the indemnity and who is required to pay it (arts. 505 and 508 CPP). But as of the moment of the writing of this report, the judge has not yet issued his rulings, the lawyers for the defense having filed a motion challenging his right to issue a sentence, based on the fact that he has been a professor at the Central American University and that this would compromise his impartiality. This attitude on the part of the defense attorneys is difficult to justify, since they knew this fact from the beginning and never filed a challenge at the appropriate procedural moment. Furthermore, the conduct of the judge demonstrated quite clearly—in the opinion of the observer—that the fact of having been a professor at the UCA in the past in no way affected his impartiality in judging the case.

Judge Zamora must also issue rulings in several other cases, which are being handled separately without the requirement of a jury, concerning the situation of four persons indicted in connection with these events: a) Lieutenant Colonel Carlos Camilo Hernández, previously Subdirector of the Military Academy, prosecuted on charges of actual concealment (art. 471 CP: removal of evidence), for having ordered the destruction and burning of registers recording troop movements to and from the Academy. These registers could have established the departure and return of the Atlacatl Battalion commandos on the night of November 15–16, 1989; b) three soldiers of the Atlacatl Battalion, prosecuted for the offense of "false testimony" (art. 464 CP), for having made untrue declarations concerning the movements of the Atlacatl on the night of the crimes.

A final event which reveals the difficult situation reigning in El Salvador is the fact that a few days after the end of the public trial, the two lawyers for the Private Accusation, Attorneys Henry Campos and Sidney Blanco, left the country to resettle abroad; they did not feel secure in El Salvador, fearing reprisals by members of the Atlacatl.

In concluding this report, the ICJ observer wishes to reiterate his appreciation to the Salvadoran authorities for having provided him with every opportunity necessary to attend the public trial. The observer was also able to move freely within the country, with a view toward getting a first-hand appreciation of the political and social context in which the trial took place.

ADDENDUM

THE SENTENCING

On January 23, 1992, Judge Zamora sentenced Colonel Guillermo Alfredo Benavides Moreno and Lieutenant Yusshy René Mendoza Vallecillos to 30 years' imprisonment, the maximum penalty under Salvadoran law. The jury had found Col. Benavides responsible for the eight murders even though he was the only one who had not confessed to participating in the acts. As a result of the verdict, the judge sentenced Col. Benavides for murder and conspiracy to commit acts of terrorism. The judge sentenced Lt. Mendoza for the murder of Celina Ramos, the daughter of the cook who was also murdered, and for actual concealment.

The jury had acquitted the seven others accused of the assassinations, despite the fact that in extrajudicial declarations they had confessed to having committed the eight murders. Three other officers, however, were sentenced for crimes which, according to Salvadoran law, are to be decided by the judge. Two of these officers were sentenced to three years for inciting and conspiring to commit acts of terrorism. The third officer was sentenced to three years' imprisonment for the destruction of evidence in ordering the burning of the logbooks. It is unclear whether the new amnesty law[1] will invalidate these sentences. Regarding Benavides and Mendoza, however, rumored attempts to include them in the amnesty have been rebuffed, at least temporarily. Appeals of the sentences are pending.

Additionally, the civil action brought directly against the accused and secondarily against the State was settled. Although the terms under which the State settled with the private complainant are unknown, the mere existence of such a settlement

---

[1] Discussed below.

implies that the State may be beginning to recognize its civil liability for the unlawful acts of its agents.

The conviction and sentencing was a first in Salvadoran history. Formerly, only FMLN members were charged with terrorism. Never before has a public hearing ended with a jury convicting a high-ranking officer of crimes constituting serious violations of human rights. Although the case reflects progress toward securing human rights, it has illuminated procedural problems in the current judicial system. For example, the jury can and did pronounce a verdict without having been present when the accused made statements and when the witnesses were examined. As a result, a broad consensus has emerged in Salvadoran society concerning the need for far-reaching reform to ensure the judicial protection of human rights and due process.

PEACE AND REFORM EFFORTS

The Peace Accord

The Peace Accord, signed in New York on December 31, 1991, represents negotiations between the State and the FMLN. Much international support of the Salvadoran government was contingent upon the adoption of the Peace Accord. Three months after the signing, however, Salvadoran human rights groups are far from praising the State's compliance with the Peace Accord. Rather, they see the Peace Accord as in crisis.

One major complaint is that the State has failed to follow the clearly established requirement of reducing the Salvadoran armed forces. The government justifies maintaining its forces by claiming that the existing violence in El Salvador is the result of the FMLN. Another complaint is that the State has attempted to appear to satisfy the Peace Accord, but such attempts in actuality fail to carry out the spirit of the Accord. For example, rather than dismantling the National Guard and the Interior Police[2] the government has simply changed their

---

[2] "Policia de Hacienda"

names to the "Frontier Guard" and the "Military Police," without changing their personnel or structure.

Amnesty

On January 23, 1992, the Salvadoran Legislative Assembly adopted the Law of National Reconciliation[3] drafted by COPAZ, the National Commission for the Consolidation of Peace. COPAZ is mandated to oversee the implementation of the Peace Accord and to form concrete proposals to carry out the Peace Accord. COPAZ is made up of two representatives of the government, one of whom is a member of the Armed Forces; two FMLN members; and one representative from each of the political parties or coalitions in the Legislative Assembly.

The LRN permits the granting of amnesty to all those persons who, prior to January 1, 1992, participated directly, authorized, and/or acted as accomplices in the commission of political crimes, common crimes related to political crimes, and common crimes committed by no less than 20 persons, excluding kidnapping. Because the legislation broadens the definition of political crimes for the purposes of this law, the amnesty includes most crimes for which FMLN members have been charged.

The new law exempts from amnesty those persons who have been convicted by a jury for any of the crimes covered by the amnesty. Thus the jury convictions in the Jesuit case should remain unaffected. Moreover, the law exempts from amnesty those persons whom the Truth Commission[4] finds "have participated in serious acts of violence which occurred since January 1, 1980, whose impact on society requires, with greater urgency, public knowledge of the truth. . . ."

Despite these exemptions, Salvadoran human rights groups have severely criticized the new amnesty law. First, although in-

---

[3] Henceforth referred to as the LRN (Ley de Reconciliación Nacional).

[4] Following the Peace Accord, the United Nations Secretary General formed the Truth Commission to examine human rights cases, chosen by the Commission, during a six-month period. Former Colombian President Belisario Betancur, former Venezuelan Foreign Minister Reinaldo Figueredo, and U.S. law professor and former Inter-American Court judge Thomas Buergenthal comprise the commission. The Truth Commission has not yet begun its work.

ternational law clearly establishes the duty of the State to investigate, try, and punish human rights violations and to compensate the victims, the LRN ignores these requirements. The LRN asserts that amnesty will allow Salvadorans to leave behind the violence of the past decade by avoiding a long drawn-out judicial process.

Second, it is unacceptable that the amnesty includes abhorrent acts, such as common crimes, committed by whomever, with the motive or reason of armed conflict, or committed by groups of 20 or more persons. Even worse, the amnesty extinguishes civil liability—the opportunity for victims to learn the truth and obtain compensation.

Third, the LRN contradicts the spirit of the Peace Accord regarding the role of the Truth Commission. The LRN does not grant amnesty to those whom the Truth Commission determines have committed "grave acts of violence." The Supreme Court has published an explanation of the application of the amnesty law, stating that judges are to abstain from granting amnesty in those cases constituting "serious acts of violence whose impact on society demands public knowledge of the truth with greater urgency" until the Truth Commission determines whether they are included in the LRN. Yet because the Truth Commission has not begun its work, the new law limits the mandate of the Truth Commission by obligating judges to confer or deny amnesty *prior* to obtaining the Truth Commission's report.

In order to avoid the granting of amnesty in cases which constitute "serious acts of violence," judges, rather than the Truth Commission, will decide which cases constitute "serious acts of violence." Moreover, once the court finds that a crime committed does not constitute a "serious act of violence" and thus grants amnesty, the amnesty is irrevocable. Thus, human rights groups find unacceptable the confusion the LRN creates regarding the Truth Commission. As a result of these problems, many groups have advertised in the press, stating that a general amnesty is premature because the Truth Commission will soon begin its work.

In conclusion, human rights groups find that the new law denies the indispensable opportunity for Salvadorans to know the truth regarding the systematic violations of human rights which they have endured for the past decade.